W0115272

Drawn by L. Pasternak

TOLSTOY AT WORK IN HIS STUDY

TOLSTOY

THE MAN

EDWARD A. STEINER

Foreword by A. N. Wilson

UNIVERSITY OF NEBRASKA PRESS
LINCOLN AND LONDON

Library of Congress Cataloging-in-Publication Data
Steiner, Edward Alfred, 1866–1956.
Tolstoy the man / Edward A. Steiner; introduction by
A. N. Wilson.
p.   cm.
Originally published: Cambridge: Riverside Press, 1904.
With new introd.
ISBN-13: 978-0-8032-9345-8 (pbk.: alk. paper)
ISBN-10: 0-8032-9345-3 (pbk.: alk. paper)
1. Tolstoy, Leo, graf, 1828–1910.   2. Novelists, Russian—
19th century—Biography.   I. Wilson, A. N., 1950–   II.
Title.
PG3385.S82   2005
891.73'3—dc22   2005014927

A. N. WILSON

FOREWORD

Edward Alfred Steiner was born into a German-speaking Jewish family near Bratislava (Slovakia) on 1 November 1866. In birth, he was a child of the Austro-Hungarian Empire, educated by his parents in the great European tradition—a public school at Vienna, a Gymnasium or High School in Pilsen, Bohemia, before enrolling at the University of Heidelberg from which he graduated in 1885. He was destined to die just before his ninetieth birthday as a much-respected and much-loved American academic, a teacher of literature for many years at Grinnell College, Iowa, and a minister of the Congregational Church. His life-trajectory is in itself parabolic, and the explanation of the parable is to be found in this, his finest book, an account, based on firsthand experience, of the great Russian storyteller and moralist Lev Nikolayevich Tolstoy.

The nineteenth century saw what the English poet Thomas Hardy called, in a memorable poem, "God's funeral." The advance of Biblical scholarship in Protestant lands undermined faith in the Bible. The geological research of Charles Lyell demonstrated beyond question that the earth and the universe were far older than the Biblical fundamentalists had supposed. Charles Darwin's theory of evolution by natural selection appeared to undermine any need to believe in a mind behind the universe or a purpose in creation. Fyodor Dostoyevsky has one of his characters, in *The Brothers Karamazov*, cry out that if

God does not exist, anything is permitted; Nietzsche proclaimed that God was finally dead.

It was in this atmosphere, which affected the whole of Europe, that Steiner came to grow up. As a student at Heidelberg, as he tells us, the "rationalistic atmosphere" was all-pervasive. And it was there that he read *War and Peace*.

As Steiner's book shows, Tolstoy himself underwent a series of religious and intellectual changes in the course of his life. His early life of sensuality as a soldier went hand in hand with a deep absorption of the works of Rousseau and an acceptance of the Enlightenment. Yet always, in the life of Tolstoy, there went, with a desire for Rousseauean simplicity, a belief in the Russian peasant. Tolstoy, when he returned to his ancestral estates south of Moscow at Yasnaya Polyana (the words mean "clear or bright glade") he experienced a sense that the men and women who worked on the land were somehow better at living than he was. Although, or perhaps because, they were uneducated, they were in tune with their inner voices; they could hear the promptings of conscience; they could still hear the voice of God. After what we should term a midlife crisis and following the prodigious success of *Anna Karenina*, Tolstoy had a religious conversion. It was not surprising that he should have tried to imitate the faith of the pious Russian peasant, by attending the Orthodox liturgy, kissing icons, and communing with the ancestral soul of Mother Russia.

For Dostoyevsky such an exercise was possible only in those moods when he overcame his natural skepticism to kneel at the feet of Jesus. But Tolstoy remained, at heart, a follower of Rousseau and a man of the Enlightenment. He believed that the Church, with its emphasis on the myths of salvation and its insistence on the miraculous elements in Christian story, was fundamentally in error. Moreover, Orthodox Christianity, which was being discarded everywhere in Europe during his lifetime, failed to answer the deepest spiritual needs of mankind: namely the question of How To Live.

The Orthodox Church, whose gospel condemned fighting, nevertheless blessed the armies of the oppressive Imperial Regime. It blessed the prisons. This church, whose gospel condemned the taking of oaths and the passing of judgement, blessed the courts that sent unfortunates on the long road of exile to Siberia. It blessed the rising bourgeoisie in Moscow and the other big cities, who took scant notice of Jesus' condemnation of those who laid up wealth. Everywhere, the simple injunctions of the Gospels—not to resist evil with violence, not to accumulate wealth, not to pursue power, were flagrantly ignored by the Christian churches. Tolstoy, with that incisive combination of rationalist directness and peasant simplicity, could see quite clearly why the voice of God was no longer heard in the nineteenth century. It was not so much because science or textual scholarship had disproved the truth of the Gospel. It was that, for many ages, the simple truth of the Gospel message had been obscured by theology and superstition. If we, as men and women, could learn to discard the pursuit of power, if we could restrain our lusts for sexual gratification and for money, if we could be pure in heart then we might, as the Gospel promises, see God. The God we should see would not be a miraculous being, capable of making the dead rise from tombs or cancelling out obvious moral evil by blood-sacrifice. It would be the inner God who speaks to everyone, giving them the assurance of righteousness when they do good and troubling them with a bad conscience when they are violent or abusive or selfish.

What *War and Peace* taught the young rationalists of Heidelberg was not a full-blown "Tolstoyanism"—the creed evolved by Tolstoy and his inner circle of disiciples after his break with the church: vegetarianism, pacifism, and so forth. It was the more direct and simple truth that within us all there is a spark of soul that cannot be explained away and that we all know to be there. Had the students of Heidelberg with whom Steiner shared his thoughts been more attentive to the works of Immanuel Kant, they might have recognized this as what Kant called the Categorical Imperative. Kant, who rejected orthodox Christianity and a belief in a personal God, nevertheless was conscious of awe at the starry skies above and the moral law within. No novelist has ever dramatized this certainty more surely than Tolstoy with his characters in *War and Peace*, such as Prince Andrew, lying on the field of battle and looking upward at the stars, or in the spiritual wrestling of Pierre, the archetypical Enlightenment rationalist who only sees the truth when watching the life and death of a simple man among his fellow-prisoners. "Life is everything. Life is God. . . . How simple and clear it is. How is it, I did not know it before?"

There is no need, therefore, to have ridiculous arguments about whether this God "exists" since only a maniac like Nietzsche's Zarathustra or his disciples among our postmodernist contemporaries could ever for a moment think that, for example, cruelty was better than kindness, or that the pursuit of power for its own sake would end in anything but tyranny and disaster.

Tolstoy's religion was supremely rational, while making an appeal to the heart. It converted, among others, Mahatma Gandhi, who was able to put into practice Tolstoy's idea of passive resistance and thereby destabilize and destroy the British Raj in India. It converted the young soldier Ludwig Wittgenstein during the First World War and opened up the mechanically minimalist philosopher of the *Tractatus* into the warmth of the later *Philosophical Investigations*.

For Steiner, the encounter with Tolstoy allowed him to leave behind the arid rationalism of nineteenth-century European thought and to embrace a mild version of the American Protestantism that had inspired the founding fathers of the Revolution. Thomas Jefferson had written a version of the New Testament that expunges the miraculous and the mythological, in very much the same way that Tolstoy was to do in his book *The Gospel in Brief*. Steiner, interestingly, from the first seems to have differed from Tolstoy in his insistent belief in life after death, a belief that plays almost no part in Tolstoy's writings but which Steiner foists on him. We all make heroes in our own image and Edward Steiner is no exception.

The great value of Steiner's book is that it was written during Tolstoy's own lifetime, and it was based not merely on firsthand accounts of what it was like to make the pilgrimage to Yasnaya Polyana and to meet the great man in person. It is written from a hero-worshipping standpoint, but it tells the story in reasonably truthful outline, making the point that Tolstoy was never blind to his own faults and never sought to hide them. It is also an account of the passionate appeal of Tolstoy's religious writings. Turgenev, as Steiner reminds us, wrote from his deathbed to beg Tolstoy to abandon the writing of tracts and to return to fiction. But as Steiner shows the great fiction, even before Tolstoy's "conversion," was soaked in the ideas that later became the novelist's overriding preoccupation.

There is a tenderness in Steiner's account of Tolstoy in old age, not least in his recognition that Countess Tolstoy, the sage's long-suffering spouse, had gone very far along the road of sharing his ideals. Steiner tactfully makes no overt mention of the terrible rows that took place between the Countess and the bigoted upholders of Tolstoyanism who surrounded Lev Nikolayevich at the last. And Steiner, of course, wrote before Tolstoy's celebrated escape from his wife and his death in the railroad station at Astapovo as he gasped, "How does a peasant die?" Steiner's Tolstoy is a gentle, tolerant fellow, not unlike Steiner himself.

Steiner went on to be an inspirational teacher. One of the Tolstoyan truths that he had absorbed even before becoming a U.S. citizen is that we are equal under God. He applied this rule more rationally than some of his fellow Americans and was an early and lifelong opponent of racism in all its crazed forms. He had a difficult time at Grinnell, Iowa, during the First World War because of his pacifism, but this did not cost him his job, as opposition to the war had cost Bertrand Russell his Cambridge fellowship.

By the end of his life, Steiner had taught nearly five thousand pupils, among them Harry L. Hopkins, the adviser to President Franklin Roosevelt who did so much to create a bond between Britain and the United States before the American entry into the Second World War.

It is strange to read Steiner's book today, when the dominant strand of American Protestantism is a form of evangelical salvationism that lays great stress on personal redemption but worries itself less about the Gospel precepts to eschew the pursuit of war and money. What drew Steiner away from arid "rationalism" was a discovery of Tolstoy's God within. What confirmed him in the rightness of his journey was his getting to know Tolstoy personally. This in turn led him away from old Europe to a land that appeared to have satisfyingly embraced the freedoms of both the Reformation and the Enlightenment. In our own day, this alliance has been broken. That is all the more reason why we should strain our ears to hear what Steiner, and his hero Tolstoy, had to say. They speak, in accents clear as still, as truthfully now as they did a hundred years since.

Dedication

" Marriage is an elevation for such as we." — *Tolstoy*

TO HER WHO HAS MADE THIS TRUE IN MY OWN LIFE, WHO
HAS GLORIFIED FOR ME WOMANHOOD, WIFEHOOD, AND
MOTHERHOOD, WHO HAS BEEN MY PATIENT HELP-
MEET IN ALL OF LIFE'S TASKS, THIS BOOK,
WHICH IS ONE OF THEM, IS DEDI-
CATED IN GRATEFUL
LOVE

INTRODUCTORY NOTE

THE author of "Tolstoy the Man," Dr. Edward
A. Steiner, who occupies the professorship of Applied Christianity in Iowa College, spent several
months in Russia at the request of The Outlook
Company and under its commission for the express purpose of obtaining material for this book.
As appears in his opening chapter, he renewed at
Yasnaya Polyana, Tolstoy's residence, an acquaintance begun many years ago. Dr. Steiner not
only had the opportunity of getting close to the
personal and individual side of his subject and
of discussing with the great Russian writer and
teacher his life and work, he brings also to his
task a study and appreciation of Tolstoy's character and theories extending over a long period.

He talked with Tolstoy's intimate friends and
admirers, was shown many letters throwing new
light on Tolstoy's doctrines and practice, gathered from newspapers and books, accessible only

in Russia, a fund of valuable facts, visited Moscow to get acquainted with the "Tolstoy circle" there, and in short used every effort to obtain all available material for an authentic and vivid memoir. It need hardly be pointed out that the personality of Tolstoy is of intense interest the world over, and this without regard to the question whether readers do or do not accept in full his social teachings. The many incidents and anecdotes here first published cannot fail to add to the world's knowledge of "Tolstoy the Man." The illustrations in the book are in part the work of the brilliant young Russian artist Pasternak, an enthusiastic admirer of Tolstoy, who has enjoyed a close intimacy with him and has painted him repeatedly as he appears in the family circle.

THE PUBLISHERS.

PREFACE

THE monotonous plain through which the Dnyper winds its way seaward is the cradle of the Slavic race. The physical character of this vast stretch, with its uninteresting moor and marsh, has impressed itself upon all the members of this widely scattered family; but especially upon the Russian, who is to-day its largest and most important member. From the lowest mujik to the highest dignitary, racial characteristics remain the same; and beneath much apparent change which wealth and culture have wrought, there is among all classes the unmistakable Slavic element. The national temperament is undisturbed by great passions, just as that cradle land is free from sudden mountain heights or vast depressions. Not unlike the land is also its history, which records no grand heroic movements in its early days. Without song or story the past lies deeply buried; and

PREFACE

although the present division of the Slavic people was not completed earlier than the seventh
century, history is silent, because no doubt there
was nothing to tell. They were at first peaceful
hunters, and after exchanging the bow and
spear for the spade, they became warriors only
when pressed to the fight. The later history
of the Slavic tribes which were surrounded or
subjugated by other races is tumultuous enough;
but in spite of the invasion of Mongol, of Swedes,
and of the French, the inner quiet of Russia
remained unbroken. The heart of this country
is like that of the ocean, — unstirred by passing
storms, — although in Russia even the surface
never rose above its appointed level. Renaissance
and Reformation alike, though they touched the
life of Bohemia and manifested themselves among
the Poles and Slovaks locked in among the cres-
cent-shaped Carpathians, passed unnoticed over
the parent nation, Russia. The Byzantine stamp
which was pressed upon its soul became a leaden
weight and the Church its prison-house, from
which neither life nor light emanated. The Ro-

man Church, while professing ardently its immutability, has given birth, though in pain, to great men who ushered in new periods; but the Greek Church remained barren. The masters of the Church — the czars, the fathers of these Russian children — were themselves like spoiled children to whom the people were playthings and the plowmen toys, such as the giant king's daughter (of whom Uhland sings) gathered in her apron and carried to her father's castle.

To the Russian the nation is a family, over which rules the God-appointed czar, whose yoke is borne patiently and uncomplainingly. He alone is capable of removing the people's burdens, and what he can accomplish has been shown by Peter the Great and Alexander II., who by a few sentences ushered in new eras for their million-headed family.

No one was born from among the people whose voice or hand was strong enough to rouse the nation from its lethargy or to make the way straight for the coming of some greater one. True, Russia gave birth to singers who struck many a brave note, but were either lured, like Pushkin, into some gilded cage, or died in exile, mute even in their last agony; others were stimulated and inspired by those vast movements which changed the political and social life of Western Europe and gave birth to a new nation across the sea; but they had no standing ground, no institution or band of men, — nothing to strengthen new-born thoughts, — and their voices died faintly away. It was thus with all the Western culture, which, in spite of passport regulations and rigid censorship, entered Russia; for it was in such great contrast to all which the State, the Church, and society tolerated that it was repelled everywhere, and had no brooding-place except among revolutionists, where it exploded, rather than grew, into maturity.

It is true that the Russian of the upper class is steeped in Western culture; but it is also true that in a large measure he has been able to get only its surface; that part of it which he found on the boulevards of Paris, on the pages of the inoffensive ladies' journals, or in books which

escaped the censor's critical eye. Much of so-
called Western culture came in with morally
bankrupt tutors and governesses who tainted
the atmosphere in which the aristocratic youth
developed and matured. One finds everywhere
genuine culture, and often more radical ideas
than in the West of Europe ; but everything is
unstable and unsteady, like isolated logs floating
in the Volga, rather than like those which have
been hewn, and fastened into a building. Out
of this condition have grown startling contrasts
between thinking and acting, knowing and
believing, between a few who are learned and the
vast mass of the ignorant, between those who
live in excess and those who have not yet begun
to live. This state of things makes the Russia
of to-day an enigma ; makes it, as Carl Emil
François says, "Half Asia," neither Europe nor
Asia. This makes it the land of the most revolutionary and the most reactionary ideas, makes
its atmosphere stifling from suppressed silence,
and vibrant from new-born thought. Some day
there will be a page in the history of Russia on

which will be written : " There was a man sent
from God whose name was " — Tolstoy, — a man
who was to break the prophetic silence of centuries, and who by plain speech and in utter self-
forgctfulness was to " make straight the way of
the Lord." His coming and his growing into such
prominence were not the trick of genius, were
not the striking of a golden vein which brought
fame and wealth to the lucky finder, but were
as truly an historic event as they were an " historic necessity." It is also true, as Eugen Schmidt
says, " that Tolstoy did not come as a preacher
of morals, as a proclaimer of a few ethical maxims which were to change the current of men's
lives, not as a man who wanted to be a good
example, not, certainly, as a philanthropist
who gave to every man who asked of him, not
as a writer of realistic novels which were to
curdle men's blood into coldness and decency ;
but he came as the proclaimer of a new philosophy of life ; a philosophy diametrically opposed
to both the philosophy of the Church and of
modern science, and 'in perfect harmony with

the philosophy of Jesus,' according to his own words."

Tolstoy's philosophy is not clear to others, although many say that it is a great light; it is by nature both mystical and rationalistic, both conservative and radical; it is both old and very new. While Tolstoy has grown out of conditions which exist in his native country, while in the largest measure he typifies the Russia of to-day in its growing contrasts, in its dissatisfaction with itself, in its spirit of cruel self-examination, and its religious nature and tendency, — he has a message for the world which he intends shall drive out a civilization based upon barbarism and cruelty; a philosophy of life which, as he sees it, is fundamentally opposed to the laws of nature, and a religion which has reduced God to the level of a Russian monarch, degraded the Saviour into a magician and the Bible into a fetish. He means to bring in a culture which shall be free from barbarism, a philosophy of life which shall be in harmony with the teachings of Jesus, and a religion which shall answer the highest promptings of the soul. He came providentially into Russia, to the Slavs, the least advanced of the civilized races, the least spoiled by modern culture; he came without sword or staff, purse or scrip, the weakest among the czar's subjects, yet stronger than the czar; and because he fights not with carnal weapons he is gaining victories for which generations might have bled in vain.

Some people may read this book because they wish to see the man Tolstoy, colossal giant that he is; and I shall try to draw him as I have seen him, and as he has impressed others who came to him in different moods and for other purposes. A smaller number will wish to find some key to his many writings, some brief account of their form, contents, and spirit, and I shall try to satisfy this demand; the smallest number will come here to read about his philosophy and his message. This last desire, too, I shall try to fulfill, although it is the hardest of my tasks. The truth is, that to do justice to the life of this man, one must touch upon all these phases; for they are part of his life. The man is in his books, and in

every line of them is his philosophy; one cannot
separate them, and yet to present them together
is a task before which a stronger one than myself might tremble. But hard though the work
may be, it is entered into with joy, because it
brings the writer again in touch with one who is
too great to be called friend, yet who is lowly
enough to call himself brother.

That I may not dim his glory, and yet not
unduly exalt him, that I may not misrepresent
him and yet truthfully present him to view, that
I may satisfy the curious and yet bring them
nearer to the source of the teachings of Tolstoy,
which is the Gospel of Jesus, — is my only desire.

My acknowledgments are due to Director
Raphael Loewenfeld, of Berlin, who placed at my
disposal his unsurpassed collection of Tolstoyana
and who marked out the channels for obtaining
new and valuable material both in St. Petersburg and in Moscow; to Eugen Schmidt, of
Buda-Pesth, who has systematized the teachings
of Tolstoy in his remarkable book "The Cultural
Mission of Tolstoy;" to Mr. Pavel Ettinger and

to various members of the editorial staff of the
" Rusky Wyedomosty," of Moscow, and to many
friends in various parts of Russia who have given
me valuable advice and encouragement when both
were needed ; above all, to Mr. George Kennan,
who is gratefully remembered by all thoughtful
Russians, regardless of their political creed, as
"The Apostle of Russia's prison reform" and by
whose thorough knowledge of Russia and Russian
affairs this book has profited as well as by his
generous and always correct criticism.

E. A. S.

Moscow, March 1, 1903.

CONTENTS

CONTENTS

LIST OF ILLUSTRATIONS

TOLSTOY THE MAN

CHAPTER I

TOLSTOY TO-DAY

TWENTY years ago there came into the rationalistic atmosphere of a German college the influence of a Russian novel which meant much to a group of young men who had thought God out of existence and had buried Christianity with all other religious superstitions. While religion seemed dead around them, it still was living within them, and the call to an heroic expression of it in Tolstoy's "War and Peace" awakened long slumbering thoughts and new and vital desires.

There must be something innate in human nature which sends men upon pilgrimages, for the first wish which the students expressed while the joy of the new-found truth had not yet spent itself, was to go to Moscow and see and hear the man who had saved them from losing a precious possession, and who had given to them a new interpretation of life and of the Lifegiver.

The young men had time, but little money, so the journey had to be made on foot, the long, most interesting trip taking them through the heart of the Slavic world. When they knocked at the hospitable door of Count Tolstoy's house in Moscow they looked more like tramps than students, and the welcome from the servants and from some members of his family was such as to send the autumn chill of the unpicturesque entrance hall into their exalted feeling. When the Count himself opened the door of the living-room, where the samovar sang and the fire crackled while the smoke of cigarettes was thick and seductive, there came with him a warm air and a warmer welcome. He was in the prime of life, at the height of his literary fame in Russia, and the larger world was beginning to grow conscious of him.

Our admiration of Tolstoy grew no less because of our close contact with him, and the spell by which he enthralled us has remained a valued and abiding possession to some of us. Neither life nor death seemed the same thing afterwards, although our minds were too immature fully to grasp his teaching and the life of pleasure was too alluring to put it off for the life of labor.

Three times this pilgrimage was made by me in maturer years, and each time the welcome was more cordial and the admission into Tolstoy's inner life more generous. These visits brought with them the privilege of meeting the men and women who see in Tolstoy not only an author and a famous man but their great teacher and the revealer of a new philosophy of life.

The winter of 1903 was spent in close relation with this circle, and while the bond with Tolstoy himself was less intimate, this was due to the fact that the news of his serious illness checked the desire of the artist and biographer to urge their presence upon him, and only after we heard that his condition had improved did we venture our request. "Come and bring N. with you," read the telegram which we received in answer to our letter. N. is a musician of note, and the feeling that through his playing Tolstoy would receive much pleasure made our going easier, for usually we felt that we gave nothing in return for the inspiration received.

To start from Moscow at midnight, to be locked

in a train whose compartments are so hot that they can well serve the purpose of a Russian bath, to inhale cigarette smoke which everywhere makes the atmosphere stale and thick, is no great pleasure, especially as the train stops longer at the stations than it travels between them, and, being the only so-called fast train, is uncomfortably crowded. No air either enters or leaves the compartment, and when we reach our destination, and can really breathe the fresh, ozone-laden air, it is as exhilarating a moment as if we had stepped from a prison cell into freedom. The little depot is almost covered by snow, and after being wakened for a moment by the stopping of the train it sinks again into the deepest quiet. Here and there from among the white birches the rising smoke tells of some mujik's cabin in which the housewife has bestirred herself and has kindled the fire. The horse and sleigh of Countess Tolstoy are awaiting us in the station yard, and almost simultaneously we ask the coachman, "How is the Count?" "Slava Bogu [Praise God], he is much better," answers the faithful servant, whose broad, good-natured face smiles at us from his wrappings of fur, which make him look like an overgrown infant ready to be carried away by its nurse. He remembers the Count's guests, and has a particular smile for those who know that Tolstoy's philosophy about money has not at all influenced his servants, who are just as eager for their tips (na tschay) as if they were living in the most materialistic atmosphere. Swiftly we glided along through the increasing quiet ; the noise of the passing train had almost ceased, and its deep breathing grew fainter and fainter. From the east a tinge of golden red poured over the silvery landscape ; for a moment there was a hovering between twilight and morning, then the sun rose, bringing light but no warmth, and the great conqueror who in the summer colors earth and skies in varied hue seemed unable to affect the mass of white or to change the great shroud into a wedding-garment. The noisy crows alone made dark spots upon the landscape and brought discord and disturbance into silence and harmony. No one in the village had yet stirred out of doors ; the peasants were still lying upon their warm bake-ovens hibernating until the spring-time, when the increasing hunger would drive them out of doors and press the plow into their hands. The snow lay up to the windows of the low cabins, which were kept from being lost in the colorless landscape by the dirt of doors and outer walls. Horses, cattle, and fowl were indoors with the peasants, and within many a hut was heard the faint cock-crow, followed by the grunting of an unfed pig or the hoof-beat of a restless horse. From above the snow, like strange-shaped mushrooms, peeped with their Chinese roofs the white towers flanking the gateway to the Tolstoy estate, and the trunks of the trees within made dark lines upon the whiteness, showing the well-worn road between them. At the door we were met by Maria Le-vovna, the Count's favorite daughter, who has been constantly at his bedside, and who at this time was acting as his private secretary and is his confidential friend. Among the Count's chil-dren the daughters had the greatest sympathy with his teachings, although since they have married they have gone the way of the world, much to his regret.

When we arrived, Countess Tolstoy was still in her room; she rises very late, her work keeping her up until past midnight. She is now correcting a new edition of her husband's works, and between the struggle with publishers and proof-readers she is taxed to the utmost, although she preserves both her youth and strength to a remarkable degree. Any one who saw her a few evenings before at the symphony concert in Moscow, radiant in a light gray silk costume, her bright eyes shining from pleasure, would not have realized how much work and how many years are burdening her.

We were immediately shown to our rooms, but great was our astonishment when we found one of them to be the Count's former study, which had been converted into a guest-room after his removal upstairs was necessitated by his severe illness. Mr. P. immediately called an indignation meeting to protest against such sacrilege, and we unanimously declared our disapproval of the change. The room should have been kept as it was. Those scattered books, that table full of loose pages of manuscript, the large ink-pot, the Count's picturesque but crude scythe, and his working garments — all are gone; the books are transferred to book-cases, where they stand like soldiers in perfect order, and our unpoetic satchels lie upon the table where he wrote all the books which made him famous. Surely there will be no holy shrine to which enthusiastic Tolstoyans may make a pilgrimage in after years, for the devastation seems complete. A physician who now is a member of the household lives in the Count's former bedroom, but the simple furniture has been left just as it was.

At the breakfast-table we find the usual contingent of strangers, and we look at one another in rather an unfriendly way, as much as to say, "What in the world brought you here to trouble a poor old sick man — can't you leave him alone?" We are good mind-readers, all of us, and we stare at each other during the informal meal, drinking our hot tea in silence ; and no friendlier look comes over the faces of these somebodies and nobodies when our party is asked to go upstairs to see the Count. The room which we enter is spacious and comfortable ; two large windows look out over the tree-tops and upon the silent fields of Yasnaya. The eye instinctively seeks the Count, and we are much startled as we see him. He is so thin that his features stand out with unusual sharpness. The eyes are still searching, but show the effect of much suffering, and a veil like the shadow of a passing cloud hangs over them. His voice, too, has grown weak, and his hand-clasp is like the touch of gloved fingers, without warmth or strength; but the greeting is not less cordial than ever. Now, struggling with approaching death, he is fastening upon paper memories and impressions of bygone years, and when every moment is precious he yet denies himself to no one, and does not stint the time which he gives to his friends. It is such a large welcome as only a large soul can give one. It is in striking contrast to the welcome which one receives from every other member of his household. Every one, from the Countess down to the guests of yesterday, makes you feel that you are here by grace alone, but he makes you feel immediately that you have done him a favor by coming. It is this natural and grateful outflow of his noble soul toward another that charms every one who comes in touch with him. Yet I cannot say that one feels comfortable so close to him. He searches too deeply. He penetrates down to the impurest motive

9

which brought you here, and you feel as if you were a thief caught in the act of breaking one of the commandments. I find that all those who come " in spirit and in truth " share this feeling with me, and I should not wonder if in the other world I see him sitting on one of those twelve thrones " judging the tribes of Israel."

The conversation first turned upon his own health. He has been near death's door ; the heart almost ceased its task of sending blood through his body, the limbs were cold and motionless, and around his bedside through many an anxious night stood loving watchers who feared the coming of a lightless morning. But no fear was his ; he was not being dragged to his grave. Calmly he awaited the moment of his departure, and he struggled neither for life nor with death. He dropped no pious phrases as he told us of his nearness to the other world ; it was the story of a traveler who came near to the gate of a city whose name and location he knew not, but of the existence of which he was quite sure. He did not tell as much of himself as we should have liked to hear; he quickly turned the conversation to the artist's and writer's work and plans, to N.'s children, whom he loves, and to all the living things which interest him so much. The praise of Yasnaya's quiet he turned into a sarcastic denunciation of the effort in the cities to build houses of entertainment for the laborers. "You take them out of the pure air into a place crowded by people, you compel them to breathe dust, dirt, and disease, and you call that helping the poor to enjoy themselves." My praise of the People's Palace in St. Petersburg, built by the present czar, found no echo in his heart. He does not believe in "throwing sweet morsels to a starving peasantry," although he was glad to hear of my observation of increasing temperance, or at least of a decrease of drunkenness, in the Russian cities where the dives have been entirely closed and people's theaters and tea-houses have taken their places.

Upon our inquisitive looks at his writing-desk, he told us that he was then hard at work writing his reminiscences, and that he had finished a new story based upon his experiences in the Caucasus, and he read us page after page of the simple but beautiful narrative from his life in those wild mountain regions. His style seems simpler than ever ; clear and sharp stand out his characters. The background is faint, scarcely touched, but the men and women whom he portrays are alive, and the truth they speak is clear and their words are pure. They are created by his love for all the men he met and knew in those young years of his eventful life.

The manuscript is as unreadable as ever, and Maria Levovna had to be called upon to decipher those passages in which her father's pen had tangled the thought of the story by successive corrections. He was greatest and most precious when he laid down the manuscript and began to tell of his own feelings and emotions in those days. How little he spares himself ! he gathers up every scrap of the past, even if by so doing he tarnishes his halo ; but he tells truth and loves truth, even if truth makes him unlovely.

We know now that the stories of his childhood and youth which were the first products of his pen were not entirely autobiographical ; that, in fact, they contained much which, while it grew in him, he did not experience in actual life. He made us all laugh by telling the story of his first dancing-lesson. He was so ungraceful that the dancing-master tied a stick of wood to his legs to make them stand out straight. "I could make better use of that stick of wood now," he said, pointing to his limbs, which were wrapped in a blanket. " But I shall surprise you to-morrow. I shall go for a walk."

After dinner, N. was asked to play. The poor musician was so nervous that he had scarcely eaten anything, and when he sat down to the piano he fairly trembled from stage fright. First on the programme were Tolstoy's old favorites, Glück, Brahms, and Händel. "They are so quiet," he says ; "their passion was lofty and never base." Mozart came next, and charmed him most, for he loves him above all the composers. He never stirs the evil and the low within us," he says of him ; " and when he touches the emotions, he does it with delicacy and purity." Chopin Tolstoy enjoys very much, and among Slavic composers he finds him the most sympathetic. During the playing of one of Beethoven's sonatas he grew visibly agitated ; and that much-condemned "Kreutzer Sonata" he heard with pleasure. Schumann's songs brought tears to his eyes. "It touched my heart so," he said, in excuse for his seeming weakness.

What a rapt listener he is, this iconoclast of art! how every fiber of his being responds to it, how he draws it in and how it intoxicates him! He knows, as did the Hebrew prophets, how art itself may become man's temple and his God, and he fights against his natural devotion to it, fearing that it might lure him from the narrow path which he has marked out for himself.

Long after the piano has echoed its last vibrant note we sit in silence and muse. The snowflakes fall thick and fast upon the already heavy-laden tree-tops, and it is winter without and within. The Count sits with his head sunk over his breast, the fingers of both hands pressed against each other, and tears in his eyes. Schumann's "Du bist die Ruh" has brought them out of his heart. Quiet, quiet everywhere but in our hearts; and is there quiet in his now that he is snowed in by old age and feels the approach of death? With peace upon his brow, there is also much pain, and such furrows seam his face as no other plow-man draws but he who comes with labor and with tears. The glow of artistic success, the gratitude of those whom he has helped into the light, — these ought to make the evening of his pilgrimage glorious. Yet each life has its trage-dies, and those of us who know realize that he will carry to the yonder side some great sorrows. His tears are for a little boy, " Vantshek," as they called him, the only one of his thirteen chil-dren into whom seemed to have been breathed the same spirit by which he was filled by the Creator. The little one looked into the world with the same clear eyes as did his father, and clung to him conscious of that inner relation-ship, the kinship of the soul. He died. The hurt in the father's heart seemed healed ; but out of the treasure of song which Schumann gave to the world, and to which he listened that afternoon, there came one tenderest note and tore open the old bleeding wound. Strangers crowd his door-way asking his blessing, and go out into the world to live as he has taught them ; strangers listen with reverence to each one of his words and be-come his disciples ; but among his own there is none to preach his message or to live it. No com-plaint has ever passed his lips, and the tragedy of his heart has no witness except his own great soul, which has taught itself to love, and in love to suffer.

His philosophy of life has not changed, his belief in the efficacy of Christ's law for the salvation of man and of society is as firm as ever, and his theological views have still the same agnostic ring; but he knows God, prays to God, loves God, and truly "loves his neighbor as himself," and does not ask, "Who is my neighbor?" It would belittle those great hours to tell all that he said and how he said it, to narrate his condemnations or write down what he approved. This was no day for a biographer to make notes or an artist to make sketches, but it was a day for men to look into the great heart of one of God's great men.

Russia knows no spring. April is still only winter painted green, and then all at once it is summer. Long, not over-straight furrows are being drawn upon the great fields which surround Yasnaya Polyana. Patient mujiks are led across the fertile acres by the more patient if not more intelligent horses; and where the wooden harrow has glided over the clods, women beat them into dust. A horseman comes from between the white-washed towers, and the peasants say one to another, "Praise God, it is our master." It is a long time since they have seen him, and a longer time since they have seen him on horseback. The rider of fast horses who renounced that luxury years ago, and walked many a hundred miles, had been lifted by servants into the saddle, as he had been lifted a few months ago from voluntary hardship into involuntary ease.

The aristocratic peasant has become an aristocratic invalid, and the man who struggled for years against the conditions in which he was born will die in the same conditions, a prisoner to environment. He deplores it, mourns over it, and laments over an unreached ideal. He still envies the peasant, who, after a hard life, will lie down upon his bake-oven and die a happy death; but as little as Tolstoy could live just like a peasant, so little can he die like one. If he had the strength, he would now, in spite of the commands and the entreaties of his physician and his wife, take the handle of the wooden plow and follow it across the fragrant upturned sod. I venture to say: "Count, you have done your plowing; you have drawn a straighter furrow and a longer one right across Russia and into the heart of Europe and the New World;" but the man who all his life has believed in his power of achievement shakes his head doubtfully as he views the work he has done.

The sower follows the plowman and the women who beat the clods into dust. Majestically, rhythmically, and slowly he walks across the black, rich earth, casting his seed, more worshipful than the village priest who scatters incense for more or less holy purposes. The sower carries his seed in a white linen sheet which hangs from his shoulder, and he thrusts his hand into it as does an artist his brush into his colors, or a generous man his fingers into his treasury. With wistful eyes Tolstoy follows his movements, quite unconscious of the fact that he has been sowing more precious seed upon larger fields; but if you call his attention to this, he will say, "The best of it was only chaff." Yet undisguised pleasure shows itself in his face when one speaks of his influence which has gone over the whole world. This very spring two American millionaires came, repeating the words of the rich young ruler and receiving the

Drawn by L. Pasternak

TOLSTOY TO-DAY

same answer, but not going "away sorrowful." Each day brings tidings of new fields upon which the seed has fallen, each day brings some ripened fruit, some apostles, more disciples, admirers most of all. If you speak to him of this, he will answer, "Thus I know that His word is truth."

Yet he envies the sower with his white sheet and his golden seed. "That man will die with nothing to regret and everything to expect," he says, and he would willingly change places with him immediately. "Why not?" he says to the astonished listener. "Is he not happier than the czar, or the emperor of Austria, or the kings of Saxony or Servia? Has he not a more guiltless conscience? Who in this world is to be envied if not he? Has he not a saner philosophy than Nietzsche, has he not a loftier theology than the Metropolitan of Moscow, has he not a healthier enjoyment of art than Wagner, is he not in closer touch with nature than millions of the wealthy who lock themselves into fireproof cages and know nature only from the railroad cars and affection only from sentimental novels?" Such is the flow of his thought each day; not so pessimistic as it sounds when coined into words, for hopefully and joyfully he is waiting for the harvest, and although he will not again be able to thrust his sickle into the ripened grain, he believes that "God's in his heaven—all's right with the world!"

He is really aged; his form is bent, his step is slow, but his vision is not dimmed. He is young and vigorous in his condemnations, and younger still in those things which rejuvenate themselves each day, and which never fail—Faith, Hope, and Love. He is still Russia's greatest living writer, in spite of the new stars which have arisen—Gorky, Tschechoff, Andrejeff. He is still the one bold, unmuffled voice which protests against the wrongs perpetrated by state and church, by czar, priest, and populace. His name is still the password which leads into the homes and hearts of all the lovers of freedom and believers in the law of Christ, but all he desires is to remain one of the Master's humblest disciples "even unto the end."

CHAPTER II

CHILDHOOD AND SCHOOL LIFE

ALL Slavic villages are alike in their unpictur-
esqueness. Draw one broad street flanked by
straw-thatched mud huts, with half-naked children in front of them, add a village pump, a
church steeple, and as fore or background a sea
of mud or a cloud of dust, and you have a
village which might stand in the Hungarian Carpathians, in Poland, or in the heart of Russia.
Such a one is Yasnaya Polyana in the district
of Krapivka, near the city of Tula. It lies not
far from the main road leading from Moscow
to Kiev, which is the Jerusalem of Russia, the
Mecca of every orthodox believer. The air of neglect which characterizes it extends to Count Tolstoy's estate, the entrance to which is marked
by two whitewashed, half-ruined towers. At the
left is an artificial pond now used by the village
women, who wash their clothes so audibly that
the woods echo from the monotonous beat of the

paddles with which they belabor the wet garments. The driveway leads through a park which has grown into a forest; leaving it, one faces a modest two-story building whose one wing is occupied by the Count and his family, while the other is a sort of city of refuge for the many named and nameless ones who seek this hospitable home. Three times in the last forty years it has received additions to suit the growing needs of the Tolstoy household, but usefulness, not beauty, was sought after and achieved, for nothing which man has done here shows the least sign of good taste, and only the shining birch and beech trees save the place from being hopelessly ugly and monotonous.

The orchard in the rear of the house has relapsed into wildness, and is almost lost in the encroaching forest. In front is a well-worn tennis-court which is of recent origin, and changes its use with the varying fashions of modern sports. On the left side of the house is a porch, large enough to be the main gathering-place of the Count's family and of his guests. One need not have a very vivid imagination to find the place melancholy; silent and secluded it certainly is, and in the

winter not far from gruesome. The estate belonged originally to the Princes of Volkonsky,
an old Russian family which traces its lineage
as far back as 1246, where it claims St. Michael,
the Prince of Cernago, as the founder of this
noble house. Maria, the only daughter of Prince
Nikolai Sergejevitch Volkonsky, brought this
then prosperous estate as a marriage dowry into
the Tolstoy family, whose depleted fortunes received through it a welcome addition, and whose
name, while much less ancient, was not less hon-
ored than that of the wealthy owners of Yasnaya
Polyana. Like many of the most virile blood of
Russia, the Tolstoys came originally from Germany, where they bore the prosaic name of Dick
or Dickman, Tolstoy being its Russian translation.
One cannot get much light upon the early family
annals, some of which, however, were dark enough
not to be boasted of by the Tolstoys of to-day.
Courtiers and politicians there were, men with
strong passions who did not shrink from dark
deeds which brought them a titled name and fortune. Of two of the Tolstoys, Ivan and Peter
Andrejevitch, we know that they held high places
under Peter the Great, although they had espoused

the cause of Sofia, and were involved in a political plot. They gained their positions by their usefulness to the monarch, who finally appointed Peter Andrejevitch Tolstoy ambassador to Turkey, where because of changing political currents he was cast into prison, and only after four years of severe suffering returned to Russia a poor man ; later, the magnanimous czar recompensed him for his hardships by new offices and grants of money. In the adventurous journey of the czar through Holland and France, Peter Andrejevitch accompanied him, rising steadily in his favor, and was finally given the delicate mission of searching for Czarevitch Alexej, who had fled from the court, and was found by Tolstoy at St. Elmo, near Naples. The czarevitch was condemned to death, and although no public execution took place, he suffered that severest penalty, presumably at the hands of this Tolstoy, who rose so high as to fall suddenly, Peter II. banishing him to a cloister near Archangel, where he died on the 17th of February, 1729. While Peter Andrejevitch left upon his family a shadow, which in the social life of the court might even be considered a halo, he also left some literary productions which show him to have had no mean talent as an author and a translator, the books he gathered in his exile vouching for his taste in that direction. This ancestor left to the present heir of his name and title the literary tendency, and no doubt Tolstoy's democratic spirit was furthered in its development by the consciousness that a great and lofty name and fame may come from very low sources. The son of this first Count Tolstoy also died in exile ; of the son whom he left, nothing is known except the fact that he was the father of one Andrej Ivanovitch, whose son began to make the name of Tolstoy renowned by great heroism in battle, and by being the grandfather of the present Tolstoy, whose fame is destined to be more lasting than his, although not won at court or on battlefield.

Tolstoy's father was what presumably all the Tolstoys were : a child of fortune, a somewhat superficial student, a fighter, gambler, drinker of fiery wine, and breaker of women's hearts. He lived up to the reputation of his class and much beyond his means, doing what many men have done before and after him, — marrying a woman who had neither youth nor beauty, but a large estate and many serfs. She helped him pay his debts, and settle down in life, so that finally he grew into as good and pious a man as she was a woman. Of her still less is known than of the father, except that she was a faithful wife, a good mother, and an earnest Christian, worthy of her illustrious son, Leo Nikolajevitch Tolstoy, who was born on the 9th of September, 1828. He was the fourth son, and was one year and a half old when his mother died. Although he never knew her, he has felt her influence all his life, and in his story, "My Childhood," mother love, that passion to him unknown, is recorded in some of the most beautiful and touching sentences which he has ever written. The mother left a new-born babe, a little girl, Maria, and only seven years later, the five children were completely orphaned by the death of their father. When this catastrophe came upon them the family had just moved to Moscow to prepare the older boys for the university. The three younger children had to return to the country home, where they were taken in charge by a distant relative, Tatyana Alexandrovna Yorgalskaya, with their aunt, the Countess V. Osten Sacken, as guardian. After her death, which occurred within four years, this duty fell upon a second aunt, Pelageya Ilinishna Yushkova, whose husband owned an estate near Kazan, where the children were brought in 1840. The change from Yasnaya Polyana to Kazan seemed advantageous to the relatives, because the latter place was the seat of a university, and again because the home of the aunt was a fashionable one, and these country-bred children might learn there the manners and ways of Russian aristocratic society. Tolstoy characterizes this relative as "a very kind and pious person, pious after the fashion of her time, performing assiduously all the rites of the Church, without being conscious of any especial duty toward her fellow men, or any necessity of a change of character on her part." She was superficial, fond of pomp and glitter, and desired for her foster children nothing beyond success at court and in fashionable society. Characteristic of her and her social circle is the wish which she expressed for her foster son, "that he might have a 'liaison' with a woman, as that gave a man a necessary experience." She also wished him to be an adjutant, preferably to the czar, and the possessor of a great number of serfs. Nevertheless, Tolstoy speaks of her to-day with filial reverence and gratitude, for she was very kind to him when at the age of about eleven years he came to her, a boy who never had a childhood, and over whose cradle hung the shadow of a sorrow which was never quite lifted. This aunt says that "he gave promise of being a very homely boy, and kept his promise so well that his looks separated him from other children, creating in him a sensitiveness which both refined and embittered his life." Everything which happened made an impression upon him and drew forth his question or comment. If his mother had lived she would have treasured that which was completely lost upon his aunts. He remembers, although dimly, far back into his child-life, and the struggles and cries of his infant years are still in his memory. He often recalls his pleasure at being bathed, and can yet feel the sensation of the smooth, warm bath-tub over which his tiny fingers moved playfully. He also recollects the first fears, the being frightened by his nurse, who, wrapped in an old shawl, came as the Russian bugaboo to frighten him and his little sister into being good children. He has a vague picture of the German tutor who was busy teaching his older brothers; but clearest of all to him is the time when he had to leave the upper rooms where he lived with his nurse and little sister Masha, and had to move downstairs where his three brothers lived. It was the step from childhood into boyhood, and when his black-haired, tender little aunt took off his baby clothes and put on him coat and trousers, it was as if she had invested him with the regalia of some burdensome station. "I could see," he says, "that she felt as I did; she was sorry for me, but we both knew it had to be; and for the first time I felt that life was not a plaything but a serious matter."

Unconsciously he began to feel an aversion to the city; for the change from the woods and fields of Yasnaya Polyana to the paved and dusty streets of Kazan was not a happy one for a boy who loved the streams and fields, the gathering of mushrooms, the chasing after rabbits, and the play with the peasant children. The oldest brother, Nikolai, came from the Moscow Univer-

sity to finish his education at Kazan, and the
two younger brothers followed a little later. They
had the best tutors that could be found ; a Frenchman, St. Thomas, later rather disagreeably immor-
talized by Tolstoy as St. Jerome in his "Youth,"
while in the same story the German tutor, Russel,
received glory and honor in the person of Karl
Ivanovitch.

The three older brothers chose the mathemat-
ical course, while Leo, somewhat independently,
chose the Oriental languages. During the years
of 1842 to 1844 he prepared himself in Arabic
and Turko-Tartaric, two languages required for
entrance examination ; but in spite of the fact
that the university authorities were rather
easy-going and could be influenced in favor of
a poorly prepared student, Tolstoy did not pass
his first entrance examination, which he took
in 1844. He failed in history, geography, and
Latin, but stood well in other languages and in
religion.

In a somewhat roundabout way it was made
possible for him to try again. This time, in the
fall of the same year, he succeeded, and with
not a little pride put on his uniform and sword,

the insignia of the university student. However, as he put his mind upon his studies with much less ardor, he failed so badly at the first half-year's examination that it seemed unwise to begin again in the same department, so he discontinued the study of languages and began to hear lectures on law. His early failure could not have been due to any lack of talent, but rather to an unwillingness on his part to grapple with dry grammatical formulae, for he showed his ability to learn classical languages long after his school years had closed. In fact he was past middle life when he studied Greek and Hebrew, but then he did it in leaps and bounds. Indeed, his teacher in Hebrew, Rabbi Minor of Moscow, says of his pupil of over fifty years of age : " He grasped things quickly, but he read only that which was of especial interest to him ; what he did not like he skipped. We began with Genesis, and went as far as the Prophecy of Isaiah. There he stopped his lessons, for to have traced in the original the development of the prophecies concerning the Messiah sufficed him. Grammar he studied only when he thought it was absolutely essential."

At Kazan he had scarcely a taste of languages, much of grammar, but most of something else which was very detrimental to study, and that was society. Kazan, a city of forty thousand inhabitants, was then the social as well as the business center of that large portion of the Russian Empire which stretched along the Volga and Kama rivers. No railroads led to either Moscow or St. Petersburg, so the aristocrats of that region made Kazan their social capital, where they spent during the winter all that their serfs had earned for them during the summer. Many a fond mother brought her daughters to find a suitable match for them, and university men were held at a premium. Formal dinners followed one another so quickly that a student did not need to provide for any meal except breakfast. After dinner a siesta was fashionable as well as necessary, for each evening brought a ball or a card party, which lasted until morning.

Tolstoy's aunt had a home, in which the busy social life made study impossible and failure at examinations a foregone conclusion. In the study of the law he was somewhat more successful than in his previous attempts, although the law faculty was the poorest imaginable, and lectures such a farce that students from other departments came to them simply to amuse themselves. Nearly all the professors were Germans who knew as little of Russia's law as they did of its language.

The student body was sharply divided between the aristocrats and the plebeians, and Tolstoy was found among his class. Even then, however, he struggled against that necessity, and began the inner battle which he did not finish until many sharp conflicts subdued his natural pride, and made him see in every man a brother. He did not win for himself comrades, and no friendships survived those years in which the making of friends is as great a privilege as the acquisition of knowledge. Those who remember him as he was at that time speak of him as a very proud and conceited young man, who was nicknamed by his fellows "Philosopher" and "Recluse." Unfortunately he found no one who could understand him or to whom he could express himself, and his critical attitude toward the coarse pleasures of the plebe-

ians, and to the more refined but just as low
pleasures of the aristocrats separated him almost
completely from his college mates, none of whom
rose above the commonplace view of life. Nasaryef, a colleague of those days, and one who was
never drawn toward him, thus describes him at
one of the private lectures on Russian literature,
delivered by a professor who walked about in
his morning gown quite unconscious of the presence of his students : "Tolstoy was one of the
most peculiar men I had ever seen ; so full of
self-importance and conceit. The professor told
something interesting about literature to which
this young man listened, and after the lecture
was over left without saying good-by." This
same Nasaryef spent twenty-four hours with
Tolstoy in involuntary confinement for having
come late and noisily to the lectures. The penalty was not very severe, and was lightened by
the fact that the Count's servant was permitted
to attend him. Nasaryef continues : —

" As we entered the jail, Tolstoy threw off his
fur coat rather angrily, and with his cap on
his head walked up and down without paying
the least attention to me. He looked out of the

34

barred window, buttoned and unbuttoned his coat nervously, and betrayed in every movement his anger over this uncomfortable and ridiculous position.

"I lay there with my head buried in my book seemingly paying no attention to what he did, although I was boiling from rage over his incivility toward me. Suddenly he opened the door and called out peremptorily to his servant, just as if he were at home, 'Tell the coachman to drive up and down in front of the window.' Then this moody and disagreeable young man stood looking out to kill time in some way. I continued to read, but the situation grew painful, and I too stepped to the window. In the street the stiff and sedate coachman drove his horse, now at a trot, and now at a walk, up and down. I said something about the beautiful stallion, — one word led to another, and an hour later we were involved in an endless discussion, the warmth of which was intensified by a mutually awakened dislike. First he gave vent to his wrath against history, in words which later he put into the mouth of one of his characters, thus : 'History is only a collection of fables and unnecessary details mixed with a lot of useless dates and names. These dates and names are the only positive things, and the rest, the death of Prince Igor, the story of the snake which bit Oleg the hero, those are fables. And who needs to know that the second marriage of Ivan the Terrible with the daughter of Tomruck was solemnized on the 21st of August, 1562, and his fourth marriage with Anna Alexejavna Kallovsky in the year 1572? That stuff I have to learn by heart, and if I do not, I get a zero in my examination. And how is this history written? All of it according to a pattern which was drawn without reason by the historians themselves. Here is an example of their teaching: "The terrible czar, of whom we have heard from Professor Ivanof, suddenly changes from being a noble, virtuous, and wise ruler, into a senseless, lewd, and cruel tyrant." Why? how? and wherefore? one is not allowed to ask.'"

Before Tolstoy left the jail, he gave Nasaryef this parting shot: "We two have the right to leave this temple of wisdom as useful and educated men; now say it honestly, what are we going to take with us into life out of this sanctuary, and of what use are we going to be to society?"

Not many young men at Kazan asked themselves or others such a question, and Tolstoy's fame as a "recluse" and "philosopher" was not diminished after Nasaryef reported this first known interview with him, in which he disclosed his views on education — views of course influenced by the peculiar conditions in the Kazan University, but views which he never changed.

Tolstoy's aversion to history was increased by his dislike of the professor who occupied that chair, and that the feeling was mutual is indicated by this correct account of an examination in his department. Nasaryef reports: "The arrival of the bloodthirsty professor is anxiously awaited by the would-be lawyers, who are almost crazed by fear. One after the other they receive their cards and answer the questions as best they can. Finally, it is Count Tolstoy's turn. I was very curious to see how he would distinguish himself, for I had already recognized in him a remarkable young man. Two or three minutes passed; I still waited anxiously while Tolstoy looked at the list, growing red and pale alternately, but remaining silent. The professor asked him to take another card, but the result was the same; he remained silent. The professor also said nothing, but looked at the badly confused student with an angry jeer. The painful scene was suddenly ended by Tolstoy, who put the lists back and walked out of the room, without looking at any one or saying a word. 'A zero; he will get a zero,' whispered the students one to the other, while I was nearly moved to tears by sympathy. The aristocrats who stood around, festively clad as if for a ball, and many of whom had to expect the same fate, told one another that a number of ladies of the highest nobility had been to see the professor, and had pleaded with him not to give Tolstoy a '1,' which meant failure. They had implored him so long that he granted their request, and gave the Count a zero, which was of course worse."

Tolstoy's dislike of history and failure in it were due no doubt to the same causes as his dislike of languages and failure in them. To study the technical part of any subject was distasteful to him; if he studied, he wanted to know just why he studied, and he preferred to solve the problems of history, rather than to trouble himself by names and dates. That he had a proper, although somewhat exaggerated, view of the faults in the teaching of both languages and history, the pedagogic development of the last twenty-five years has proved. In languages we show to-day the body before the bones, the living language before the rigid frame, the grammar. In history we find the wherefore of the event more important than its correct placing in the calendar. Only one professor at Kazan knew how to attract this early ripe mind, and that one was Professor J. D. Meier, who lectured on civil law. He won Tolstoy by assigning him the work of comparing the "Sketch of the New Code of Laws of Katherine the Great" with Montesquieu's "L'Esprit des Lois." This was the kind of work now largely carried on in modern universities, and known as the "seminar." But it held Tolstoy's complete attention, and proved his only successful and profitable work at Kazan. What he was to experience as a man had already begun its premonitions in his soul. He had commenced climbing the mountain, whose height he was to reach through self-denial; although every moment his feet were slipping, and he seemed to have lost his faith and all foundations for a moral life. That which has made so many slip and fall never to rise again, the difference between the professions and the practice of Christians, was already his stumbling-block; and his aunt's pious prayers and impious ambitions, her singing of heaven and helping to create around her a social hell, were not the least of the causes which drove him to a complete bankruptcy of faith; so that when he was eighteen years of age he had lost all of God that he brought with him into this world from the other. "I remember," says this treasurer of his own childhood's thoughts, "when I was eleven years old, how a schoolmate came to me and told me that there is no God, and that we all received this statement as a piece of strange news; something possible but not probable. Furthermore, I remember," he says, "how I went walking along the lake in the springtime, on the day of my examination, how I prayed to God that I might pass successfully, and I recall how, after I had learned the catechism, word for word, I knew that it was all untrue." Suddenly he came to his conclusions

YASNAYA POLYANA

Drawn by Charles W. Furlong

and decision, and threw things overboard, only to weight himself immediately, by new problems.

Thus at the age of sixteen years he was already fighting a moral battle within himself and was trying to find some solid basis for his lofty and wandering thoughts. Alone, under the beeches of Yasnaya Polyana, during long vacations, he went through the real schooling which he sought. The old and the new philosophy, fugitive volumes from the classics, and the moderns, who began to move and think, were his teachers, while at the same time he tried to bring them all to that highest of tests, already unconsciously established in his life, — the law of Jesus, which to him was to be the only law. Like the One who was to be his Master, he was among the teachers asking questions, and had he been in the school of Athens, or at Jerusalem, rather than in the stiff, cold atmosphere of Kazan, he might have learned more and scorned much less. He lost himself in thought, and finally, by thinking about his thinking he entered into an endless labyrinth, and began that self-analysis, that hard reasoning, which rested completely upon reason and yet broke from it at every point. His university studies were never completed, and while he may not have known more than his teachers, as he at one time claimed, he knew better than they, or at least he honestly determined to know better, even if it led him away from the usual sources of knowledge. His brothers had finished their courses at the university, and he found himself more alone than ever. He was at that time like a volcano, thrown out upon the Russian plain, and asking the reason for his being and the end of it all; he was conscious of his isolation, conscious of some strange light, some burning fire, yet he began to realize that it was wrong for him to stand upon his height, to consume his fire or be consumed uselessly by it. As little as he was at home in the university, so little was he at home in that society of which his aunt's house was the center. He was roughly made, sharp-eyed, and angular in speech and movement. He says of himself, "I was shy by nature, but my shyness was increased by the consciousness of my homeliness. I am satisfied that nothing so determines the direction of a man's life as just his exterior, whether he is attractive or not." Wherever Tolstoy draws himself he makes himself as unattractive and shy as he really was. This lack of personal beauty may have helped him to break suddenly from that society which never held him, but which was to reach out her seductive arms to him again and again and keep him awhile in her embrace.

Pushed aside or having stepped aside, or both, he had a fine vantage-ground from which to watch the hollowness and the folly of it all; the ungenuineness of its affection, the madness of its whirl, and the horror and degradation of its aim and end. He had a passion to be good, to find a kindred soul with kindred longings, but if he expressed such a thought he was laughed at. He says, "When I gave myself up to ignoble passions they praised me : I was encouraged in being conceited, domineering, angry, revengeful. All that was highly commended." After more than thirty years he said in his "Confessions" : "I cannot think of this time without fear, repugnance, and heartache; in every fiber of my being I wanted to be good, but I was young, I was passionate, and I was alone whenever I sought the good." Yes, he was alone as all the seekers are ; he was in a narrow path, where the two or three seldom walk together, but each for himself passes through the temptations in the wilderness. On the 12th of April, 1847, Tolstoy petitioned the dean to permit him to withdraw from the university on account of his health and his personal affairs. On the 14th he received his papers and soon after left Kazan for Yasnaya Polyana.

CHAPTER III

THE LANDED PROPRIETOR

TOLSTOY did not enter upon his work at Yasnaya Polyana without meeting the opposition of his aunt and the ridicule of his brothers. In that autobiographical sketch, "Mornings of a Landed Proprietor," he speaks frankly of his experiences at that period. The hero of the story writes his aunt of his determination to live for the peasants, whom he has found in a wretched condition, out of which he feels that he must save them, a work which seems to him more necessary than the continuation of his studies, and which he can do without academic training or a university diploma. He closes the letter by saying : " Do not tell my brother ; I am afraid of his ridicule."

The aunt in the story, who no doubt represents his own relative, replies : " I have grown to be fifty years of age, and known many respectable people, but I have never heard that

45

a young man of good family and much talent
should bury himself in a village under the pre-
text of doing good to the peasants." The Russian young men of good family were living off the
peasants, and not one of them had yet dreamt of
living for them. The peasant was a serf, not
much better than an animal in the estimation of
his owner, and the nobler instincts of both lord
and serf were crushed, or remained undeveloped
by that nefarious institution, slavery. Most of
the land-owners lived in the cities or traveled in
foreign lands, where they spent even more than
could be earned for them by the serfs, left in
charge of unscrupulous managers, who ground
out of them all they could; and in the grinding
process both the nobility and peasantry came
near irreparable ruin. The slavery in the South
of our own country had similar yet different
effects, because in Russia the slaves were of the
same blood as their masters, with only a superficial culture and the right of possession to dif-
ferentiate the two classes, so that the reflex action
was immediate and severe. Tolstoy discovered
the danger to both, and recognized in the peasant
his kinsman, simple and unspoiled, who needed,

as he thought, but to have his faults pointed out to him, to remedy them quickly and completely. He went to his task with a holy enthusiasm and with no little heart-searching as to whether after all he was not doing it selfishly and with a desire to be odd, two faults of which he was always conscious and against which he was manfully struggling. He went to Yasnaya Polyana because he wished to give to his life a purpose which could be an answer to the question that was always ringing in his ears : "Why am I in the world?" Here in this ruined village, among these peasants, with centuries of woe upon their shoulders, he would work as a redeeming force. "I have thought much about my responsibilities in the future," he says in that letter to his aunt. "I have set up certain maxims for my actions, and if God will give me life and strength, my plans shall be carried out." No doubt the desire to live among the peasants was fostered by the reading of Rousseau, who made such a great impression upon Tolstoy that he now says of that period : "I idolized Rousseau to such an extent that I wanted to wear his portrait on my breast beside the saint's picture."

Tolstoy worshiped Rousseau, largely because he recognized in him one whose spirit was akin to his, and because Rousseau expressed plainly what was as yet confused in his own brain ; the feeling that something was wrong, that the contrasts in society were too great, that the culture which he saw and in which he lived was only a varnished barbarism : these things he had felt for a long time, and Rousseau's call for a return to unspoiled nature harmonized with his feelings and found a ready response.

Tolstoy's course also caused much shaking of heads among the peasants, who could understand his attitude even less than did his aristocratic relatives. To the peasants the coming of the owner of Yasnaya Polyana was always something to be feared, for it meant that money had run low, that debts were pressing, and that new methods of getting money out of the serfs and out of the soil had to be invented. They used to be called before the master to hear of additional expenses which they must bear, and with threats and curses to have loaded upon them burdens which grew so heavy that the poor creatures became benumbed even to any feeling of grief or opposition. Now they were called together on Sundays to unburden themselves, to bring their complaints and ask for such assistance as they might need. They were always suspicious of their masters, but when one came with kindness they were still more so. They were always told untruth and they answered in the same coin; they were robbed, and in return they stole whatever they could; they and their masters lived in two worlds, each unknown to the other, and were not only estranged but antagonistic. All the elaborate system which Tolstoy organized to uplift them the peasants regarded only as a new method of getting more work and more money out of them, so that the experiment had to fail and did; not only because they were suspicious. It failed also because the peasants are naturally impassive and do not even now care to be disturbed. Tolstoy built them model houses into which no one would move, even out of huts which might at any time bury their inmates; huts which were damp and dark and not as comfortable as some stables. Yes, the peasant asked for wood to repair them, and if it had been given him, he probably would have sold it or used it for firewood; but to move into a new house, sanitarily built, — "no, indeed not, they are veritable fortresses, not homes." Home to him was a broken-down shack, the unused manure lying about the door, another hut in the same condition, leaning in a neighborly and confidential way against his, and the odoriferous village pond right under his nose. "Leave us here," the peasants pleaded, "do not drive us out of our nest into a strange world," — the strange world being not a mile from the center of the village. "Why don't you fertilize your field?" Tolstoy asked a peasant who was complaining about his own poverty and that of his soil. "Your honor," he replied, "it isn't the manure which makes the grain grow, but God; God does everything." At every point Tolstoy was met by poverty, lies, and an unwillingness or inability to respond to most generous help. The school he built remained empty, the model houses were uninhabited, while the peasants remained just as they were, and perhaps lazier if not less honest because they had been met by gentleness and love. It was not a feeling of disappointment which filled Tolstoy at his failure, but rather a feeling of shame that men could be so crushed

by adverse conditions that they could not feel
kindness or respond to it, and that a life of self-
denial for the sake of others should be such an
impossibility. He began to realize the distance
between himself and those whom he desired to
help, and to feel that the only way to reach
them would be to change the relation between
master and servant, and himself become "like
him that serveth." His experiences also suggested the question, whether, after all, the peasant's life is not the best one ; whether the serf
who works hard and sleeps off his weariness in
the fragrant hay is not the happier man ; and
whether that half vagabond and half peasant,
"Ilyushka," who harnesses his horses and drives
from city to city seeing land and people, earn-
ing his chance ruble and spending it for food
and drink, — whether his life is not the happier
one ; and he closes his reflections by saying:
"Why may I not be like Ilyushka?" He already
begins to think about sinking himself into his
people, but the desire to know more draws him
to St. Petersburg, where he halts among many
opinions, now wishing to enter the government
service as an official, and again planning to join

the army on its way to Hungary, where it is to
help Austria in the suppression of a good-sized
rebellion. Finally he enters the university, listens indifferently to lectures on law and passes
some kind of examination, without having studied
anything; for he spends the nights carousing
and the days sleeping, and deadening his conscience by drink. In the spring of the year 1849
he returned to Yasnaya Polyana, not as a reformer, but as a man who needed to be reformed.
This time he did not come alone; he had picked
up in St. Petersburg a piece of wrecked humanity, a German musician whom he found on the
outer edge of society, ready to drop to his ruin,
whom he carried home to nurse back to health.
With him he began enthusiastically the study of
music, and was initiated into the mysteries of
the German tone-world, to which he had been a
total stranger. He had known only that music
which Russian society cultivated, which was as
superficial and as light as its own moral fiber.
Now he learned to love the severe and express-
ive qualities of Bach, of Gluck, and of Beethoven, becoming a passionate lover of the latter's
compositions. About this time Tolstoy's brother,

TOLSTOY THE MAN

Sergei, came into the tuneful atmosphere of Yasnaya Polyana, but as a disturbing element, for he was passionately fond of gypsies, and brought a horde of them to make merry for him and his companions. The Russian gypsies are professional merry-makers, and although poor, are a rather expensive luxury, which only the rich can afford. They are found in nearly every pleasure resort in Moscow, picturesquely clad, swift and graceful in their movements, dancing wildly and singing joyously, the women with their dark and fiery eyes kindling the sluggish blood of the pleasure-loving Russian aristocracy. The gypsy is never sorrowful, for he has no history to sadden him by its defeats, no prophets to burden him by their mission, and no moral code to give inconvenient twinges to his conscience. He is the best plaything that a Russian noble can find, although not seldom proving his moral and financial ruin. Sergei married one of these gypsy women, and almost persuaded Tolstoy to do the same thing. Yasnaya Polyana came again into its former glory; there were wild music, dancing, gambling, and hunting; sleigh-rides behind fast horses, excursions to

53

Moscow, and debauches which lasted for weeks, with scarcely any time between to become sober. In the two years since Tolstoy's failure as a reformer, his beautiful dream of being with nature and living for others had changed into a horrible nightmare of vulgar excesses, and he himself had sunk to the level of a common gambler in whom the passion had grown to be almost a mania. Vainly did the oldest brother, Nikolai, who was much devoted to him, try to persuade him to enter the army and go with him to the Caucasus; he preferred the "broad" life of Moscow where he could "eat, drink, and be merry," and let the morrow take care of itself. Nowhere in the world is sin quite so seductive as it is in and around Moscow, unless it be in Paris; but there one reaches bottom much sooner, and a sensitive conscience quickly begins its accusations. In Moscow pleasure comes with oriental sweetness and gentleness; it rocks the conscience to sleep while it keeps the passions awake. Moscow holds one in her warm embrace as if she were a rich and delicate fur coat which shields from cold and hardship; she spoils one for life without making one dissatisfied by it.

TOLSTOY THE MAN

Moscow has a Puritanism of form, but not of conscience; she has countless churches and no preachers. The worst excesses are not only tolerated by society but also encouraged, and had it not been for Tolstoy's ever-accusing conscience, and his keen, self-analyzing mind, he would have gone to the bottom, without, of course, losing his place at the top. There are elegant mansions on Moscow's boulevards whose purpose is not quite known to the uninitiated. Until daybreak restless horses and patient coachmen wait in front of them for their masters, who come out sobered by severe losses or doubly intoxicated by excessive drink and their winnings at games of chance. At such places Tolstoy was a frequent visitor and a constant loser; with dogged determination he placed his fortune upon the whirling wheel until heavy debts pressed him sorely, and the sham and the shame of it all drove him one day back to Yasnaya Polyana, and from there to the Caucasus. He desired to run away from a society which was so attractive and yet so repulsive, which had exacted from him its tribute, and had now so grievously burdened him by its dubious reward.

CHAPTER IV

THE CAUCASUS

"THEN why did you come to the Caucasus?" Tolstoy asks one of his characters, who answers: "Do you know why? because in Russia we believe that the Caucasus is a country for all sorts of unfortunate people, but oh! how disappointed we all are!" "I am not," the interlocutor replies; "I love the Caucasus now more than ever, but in a different way."

This last phrase rightly expresses Tolstoy's attitude toward that country. He did not love it as Lermantoff and Puschkin loved it, for its scenic beauty, for its virgin snow, for its laurel and acacia, for the sweet notes of its nightingales, for the possibility of forgetting and being forgotten; he loved it and still loves it because here in this utter desolation he " came to himself." Here was the prodigal's first " far country," in which " no man gave unto him." Here he learned to know that large and sorrowful company, the ills of the human race, — hunger, cold, hardship, sickness, danger, death, and fear of death. To him nature spoke in human terms; in its beauty and power, in its heights and depths he saw the divine forces; not as opiates for dreams and artificial ecstasies, but forces for human redemption. He was not moved to a glorification of that which was already glorious, and in a night when he felt all those mysterious sounds melting into an harmonious quiet, " when all the manifold, scarce audible movements of nature which one can hardly grasp or understand, flowed together into one full, majestic voice which we call the silence of the night," which men disturbed by the preparation for battle, he asked himself: " Is it really so hard for men to live in this glorious world, under this immeasurable, starry sky? Is it possible that in the midst of this enchanting nature, the human soul can harbor feelings of envy and revenge or the desire to exterminate a like being? It seems to me that all the evil must disappear out of the heart at the touch with nature, that immediate expression of the beautiful and the good."

In the year 1851 Tolstoy came to the Caucasus, burdened by his conscience and his debts. He lived

in the simplest way possible, among the people, to
whom he now gave himself as utterly and unself-
ishly as he had given himself in Yasnaya Polyana.
He paid five dollars a month rent for a peasant's
isba, lived on black bread and the meat which he
brought from the hunt, and listened ardently to
the simple speech of his companions, drawing for
mental and spiritual strength upon everything
which touched him. In company with a simple-
minded Cossack he tramped through isolated regions; and one day after having caught a hawk
(which is used in the Caucasus for hunting purposes), and being much elated over it, he came
quite unexpectedly upon an officer who proved
to be his near relative and an adjutant to the
commanding general. He persuaded Tolstoy to
take service in the army; and after some difficulty
with the authorities about his papers, he passed
the necessary examination at Tiflis and donned
the soldier's uniform. He became a non-commis-
sioned officer in an artillery regiment which was
stationed on the Terek River, a tumultuous mountain stream, on whose shores lived an equally un-
tamed and rebellious people, the natives of the
Caucasus, who always "fought for freedom on

the heights." They carried on an unsuccessful guerrilla warfare which kept the Russian army busy for decades, and gave many a young soldier his baptism of fire. Although the service was dangerous and at times arduous, it did not keep the busy mind of Tolstoy sufficiently engaged. Much as he loved the wild life he lived and the close touch with the Russian soldiers, of whom he was always fond, he was tortured by homesickness; and Yasnaya Polyana with its white birch forests, its gentle undulations and its simple peasant folk was often before his eyes. It was perhaps natural that when death so often stared him in the face, he should think much of his childhood and that he should desire to fasten these pictures upon paper. So he wrote his first story in a soldier's tent, little dreaming of his literary career or the success of these simple memories of his early years. On the 5th of July, 1852, he sent the story "My Childhood" to St. Petersburg, where it was immediately accepted as the first attempt of a great genius who later verified all expectations. On the 25th of November he received a very encouraging letter from his publisher; and by the light of the camp-fire he saw himself proclaimed a successful author, although without pay, for there was no check inclosed.

He had not waited to hear the fate of his first work, but by this time had already sketched "The Mornings of a Russian Land-owner" and "My Boyhood," the last named to be a continuation of "My Childhood" and part of a long story in autobiographical form which was to reach its culmination in "Manhood." This work, however, was never completed.

The period in which Tolstoy began his literary career was an important one in the history of Russian letters. Dostoyefsky, Gogolj, and Turgenieff had dipped their pens into the blood-drops of the serf and the exile, and had written in a prophetic way of "the hurt of my people." They had cut loose Russian literature from the romanticism of Schiller and Byron, and had given the world pictures, not of the passions of the flesh, but of the thralldom of "Dead Souls." So the way was prepared for Tolstoy, and his star rose upon a night which already had written upon it the prophecy of a brighter morning. "May God grant Tolstoy a long life, and I hope he will surprise us yet, for his is a talent of the first order." So wrote Turgenieff to a friend, at the time of Tolstoy's début as an author. Indeed, this first effort, which scarcely can be called a story, had in it not only the prophecy of greater things, but also their foundations. With truth and sincerity he struck the first note about the self and the inner life, and it vibrates in all his works with growing strength. This is as rare in literature as it is in life; but the desire for an open confession, for perfect self-examination and purification, which is so characteristic of Tolstoy's literary life, manifests itself in this, his first work. The little boy, Nikolenka, stands at the coffin of his mother and thus describes his feelings: "I was very miserable because my new coat, which they had put on me, was so uncomfortable around the shoulders; I was careful not to get my trousers dusty, and I stealthily examined all my surroundings." Older people than Nikolenka have felt the same way, but they have never confessed it. The contrast which Tolstoy has drawn between the Princess Kornakova, Prince Ivan Ivanovitch, and the common people around them; the half-educated tutor, the peasant Grisha, and the dear old nurse reveal that love and appreciation of the "other half" which has given to his life its direction, and has made him the revealer of the Russian mujik.

Another characteristic of his later works also manifests itself here, in his hatred of commonplace phrases: he loves and admires the genuine. Nikolenka, the hero of his first story, says: "The words of comfort, that it is well with her over there, and that she was too good for this world, — roused in me the feeling of anger." But in the corner of the hall he sees the old nurse kneeling; she does not weep, but mutely stretches out her hand toward God; and he realizes that she alone loved his mother truly. He goes to her and finds comfort because she is really bowed by grief, and is not mourning to be seen by others. Speaking of her death, he says: "She dies peacefully, without regret and without fear, because she has retained her simple, childlike faith, and because her life has been according to the law of the Gospel, with all its sacrifices and labors."

Thus early, Tolstoy recognized the spirit of that Gospel whose herald he was to be, and

TOLSTOY PLOWING ON HIS FARM

which he also would try to live in all its simplicity and with all its rigor. Yet, unconscious of the great future before him, he asked himself at the close of the story of his childhood, " Has Providence united me to these two souls only to let me mourn for them ? "

The next story, " Mornings of a Landed Proprietor," was still only a picture of his own soul life into which the portraiture of other characters scarcely entered. It was to remain practically the groundwork of all his stories; as he was to tell only what he saw with his own eyes and felt in his own heart. He experienced everything which happened to his characters; and instinctively, one feels that what he has written is in a large measure the autobiography of his own soul. In the " Mornings of a Landed Proprietor" he shows us the first noble passions of his life, and to purify that life by self-denial and sacrifice, to become a stepping-stone for his neighbor's good, to enter into the huts and hearts of the lowly, these are the first struggle, the first great battle in which he is driven back, but not defeated.

Although there was the momentary reaction

in his aspirations, he finds in the Caucasus his full strength, and his soul again rises Godward ; in spite of towering mountains, his keen eyes see the poor, struggling mountaineer; and in spite of the battle, where drums beat and flags wave, he sees nothing but the soldiers, and hears nothing but the voices of the living, who are soon to die. Thus his stories from the battles in the Caucasus plainly show their deep human interest. In "The Sortie, the Story of a Volunteer," the only story of the Caucasus which he completed there, Tolstoy tenderly and sympathetically draws the Russian soldier with all his faults and virtues. In Captain Chlopoff, who came up from the people, he personifies the genuine Russian soul, uncomplaining, not boastful, and perfectly honest. The captain serves in the Caucasus, as he frankly confesses, not because of his love of war or of honor, but because of the war pay, with which he supports an aged mother and his only sister. When he defines bravery as "doing what one ought to do," Tolstoy's sarcasm strikes the man who is vainly boastful. In contrast to the Frenchmen who have uttered memorable words in the

face of death, he says : " Between their bravery
and the captain's there is this difference : in
case a lofty thought should move in the breast
of my hero, he would not express it ; first, because of a fear that if he uttered the great
word he might spoil the great work ; and secondly, because when a man feels in himself
strength for a great work, he finds words su-
perfluous." In this story Tolstoy draws for the
first time the horrors of war ; and already we
recognize in him a soul which, although brave,
and without fear of death, shrinks not only from
the suffering of others, but even from describing it. The first bullet that strikes human flesh
immediately destroys for him the interesting
picture of the battle. "Why should I tell the
details of this terrible spectacle," he asks, " when
I would give much to forget all about it myself?" Yet with a few broad strokes, without
much color or detail, he tells us everything. A
young lieutenant just from the school bench,
with the traditional idea of bravery in his mind,
throws himself at the foe hidden in the forest.
He is accompanied by about thirty soldiers, who
soon come back, carrying the wounded officer. To

the encouraging jests with which he is met by his comrades, he scarcely gives an answer. The surgeon, ready for work, rolls up his sleeves, and with a stereotyped smile says : "It seems to have blown a hole into your skin ; let us see." The lieutenant tries to sit up, but the look which he gives the physician, although unnoticed by him, is full of surprise and accusation. The surgeon begins to examine the wound from every side ; but the injured man loses his patience, and pushes his hand back with a heavy sigh. "Leave me," he says, in a scarcely audible voice ; "never mind me, I am dying ;" and in five minutes this first tragedy of the battlefield is over.

Still deeper out of his Caucasus experience Tolstoy drew two other sketches : " The Wood-cutters," and "The Meeting with a Moscow Acquaintance." In the first story he sharply characterizes the Russian soldiers and divides them into three main classes : the obedient, the commanding, and the reckless. He uses the story to draw each class, doing it with such skill that we at once feel ourselves acquainted with all of them. He does not analyze or describe the character, but he shows us the man through a word

which he speaks or the work which he does. In
the second sketch he describes an aristocratic
youth, fallen to the lowest level, with all manhood crushed out of him by his vicious life.
This is a type not rare in Russia, and which
may be found wherever the scum of society
settles. Nechludoff, the narrator of the story,
had met this youth three or four years before,
in the home of his sister, which was one of the
best in Moscow ; and this short time had sufficed
to bring him so low that now he is a drunkard,
a companion of the lowest camp-followers, and
quite incapable of thinking an honest thought.
Tolstoy has often in later stories pictured just
such cases, in which men fell suddenly from the
highest planes of culture to the lowest depths,
and he always shows that keen insight which
comes from personal experience and contact with
those unfortunate and sinful ones, who found
him ever ready to help and to sympathize. In
his portrayal of such men, one always feels
that although he does not spare them in de-
picting their faults, their deep, inner decayed
self, he does it with the thought, " it might have
been I ;" and one cannot despise them, although

they are far from lovable. Moreover, they are to represent a class, that higher class of Moscow and St. Petersburg, where culture is at its best and worst, where lives are crushed out politely, where fortunes are ruined suavely, and where character is destroyed without breach of etiquette. Tolstoy puts such people beside the poor and ignorant, who have not lost their better selves in houses of many rooms, but have lived in huts, close to the soil and close to God. They did not search for glory, neither did they yield up life in dishonor. How magnificent is that poor common soldier, "Velentzuk," who in his death agony draws out his pocket-book, and wants to pay his debts ; who, always honest, wishes to leave this life an honest man still. There is no hypocrisy about this; it is done simply, naturally, and in strong contrast to those aristocratic officers who can speak in two languages and not keep their word in one.

Although in these stories Tolstoy deals with one subject, war, and with one class, the soldier, he does not describe war as a massing of troops, a march and countermarch, but rather as a struggle between individuals. Although the battlefield

which he describes in other stories is greater
and the strife involves nations, he never loses
this peculiarity which gives his stories such charm
and adds not a little to their horror. Moreover,
he is never intoxicated by powder smoke, by the
waving of flags, or by the fervor of patriotism;
he does not gloat over the slain of the foe, nor
does he weep over a lost cause. He sees war as
one might see it who belongs to both sides;
and to him blood and tears have the same color,
no matter under what flag they are shed.

Confessedly out of this Caucasus period, though
written much better, comes his first long and well-
rounded story, "The Cossacks." Most of the incidents in it were told him by an officer during a
night's journey, but he has concentrated everything upon his hero, in whom we quickly recognize
the author himself. Olenin, as the hero is called,
is a youth of twenty-four years who has learned
much, but knows very little; who has planned to
do great things and has never accomplished anything. At the age of eighteen, he had no burdens,
no responsibilities, and gave no bounds to his
physical and moral excesses. He had faith in nothing, and hoped for nothing; he had no family,

no God, and no fatherland. He did not believe in women, yet hungered inwardly for love; he looked down upon earthly honor, yet was glad when a prince spoke to him. He devoted himself to art, to society, and to work only until it became labor. Suddenly he drops everything and goes to the Caucasus, drawn by visions of fair women, high mountains, and freedom; and there, far away from his Moscow acquaintances, he begins the new life, conscious that the old one was wrong and that he has lived to no purpose. He comes into the home of a Cossack officer, makes the acquaintance of his beautiful daughter, and promptly falls in love with her. He also meets her lover, Lukashka, the bravest young Cossack of the camp; and above all, he gains the friendship of the hunter, Yeroshka, whose simple philosophy of life so impresses him that he decides to throw off everything of the past and remain in this wilderness. Nevertheless, he realizes that his aim in life is other than theirs, and that an unbridgable gulf divides them. He learns this through Maryanka, the girl whom he passionately loves, but who cannot in the least respond to his feelings, so he leaves the camp, and as his troyka is about to start, Maryanka steps to the door without showing the least sign of emotion.

Two thoughts which began to manifest themselves in his first story come out strongly in "The Cossacks," and increase in power in every one of his future works. First, the purification and development of the self through casting off the prejudices and evil effects of our culture; and secondly, that where such culture has not penetrated, we find the virtues which society must make its own for the sake of its true growth and salvation. These two thoughts he brings out everywhere in the same way — the first by that sharp analysis of the self in which he sees not only himself but all the people of his class caught in the same meshes, spoiled by the same culture, and whom he unsparingly analyzes, probes and condemns. The second thought he develops by drawing the characteristics of the common people whom he sees unspoiled, as they came from the hands of the creator. As a sculptor who finds the proper clay and tenderly and firmly touches and moulds it, he uses this coarse material to show what in it is lovely; yet forgetting that, like the sculptor, he himself often creates that beauty.

CHAPTER V

SEBASTOPOL

IN 1853 Tolstoy left the Caucasus, more dissatisfied with himself than ever. Love and war had destroyed the quiet and the peace which he had enjoyed the first few months, and his awakened and appreciated talent had worked havoc with his decision to live always among the Cossacks. The desire for self-effacement gave place to a conscious craving for an audience, and he left the lonely mountain regions for Moscow and Yasnaya Polyana. He found Russia on the eve of the Crimean war, which brought so little glory to the victors and so much untold suffering to all the nations involved in it. Tolstoy asked to be reassigned to the army, and it speaks much for his courage that he asked to be sent to the division on the Danube which was then face to face with the opposing Turk. After a brief visit to Yasnaya, he went by way of Bukarest to his regiment, where in its attempt to keep Omar Pasha from crossing the Danube it suffered its first defeat. Tolstoy was also present at the siege of Silistra, where Turkish soldiers under German officers, after defending the fortification which was almost blown to pieces, drove the besieging army across the Pruth and the Danube. From Silistra he went to Yassy, and from there to the Crimea and the besieged Sebastopol which was the center of the war, the gateway into Russia. Before its walls the allied armies of England, France, Sardinia and Turkey lay for eleven months, struggling with the resistant Russian soldiers, who, behind the earthworks thrown up hastily, fought bravely and with renewed zeal, in spite of the never-ceasing and murderous fire of the enemy.

In three sketches, "Sebastopol, December 1854, May 1855, and August 1855," Tolstoy describes his experiences during the eleven months of the siege, during which he was commander of an artillery brigade and present in every important engagement. He leads the reader through the city while it has not yet quite lost its semblance to a place of residence for human beings ; he sees the scattered reminders of war, the stranded ships in the harbor, the ruins of the Russian fleet, sunk to bar the waterway for the enemies' vessels, soldiers marching to their new post to relieve some worn-out, decimated regiment, or, saddest sight of all, a Tartar's cart loaded heavily with the bodies of the slain, carried to their last resting-place without honor or ceremony. From afar, like the roll of thunder, comes the noise of belching guns, and he cannot help a momentary feeling of pride that he, too, is in Sebastopol. The war which he was now to experience was to change somewhat his view of the Russian officers, for here they were not adventurers, as in the Caucasus, but defenders of the Fatherland, and he sees the same feeling of earnestness and devotion in the driver of the cart, the common soldier, and the white-gloved officer. Upon the streets there is nothing to prove the necessity for extraordinary valor, but he leads us immediately into the hospital, a former clubhouse ; he opens the door, and we shrink from entering, for we are driven back by the spectacle which presents itself and by the odors which penetrate our nostrils. "But go on," he says ; "unfortunate people like to see a face which pities them ; " and he leads us bravely from bed to bed while hesitatingly he enters into conversation with one and another of the patients. "Where are

74

you hurt?" "In the leg," is the answer, and we notice that the leg is gone. Simply the soldier tells the story of his wounding, but omits the fact that after he was shot he refused to leave the ranks until he saw whether the guns which he had helped to load did some damage to the enemy; and that in spite of his lost leg he is eager to go back to teach the young soldiers how to shoot. Farther and farther we go, until we reach the operating-room and come face to face with the real tragedies of war, after which he stops, and says: "You will witness terrible and heart-rending scenes, you will see war, — not in its scientific, beautiful, and glittering order, with bugle-call and drum-beat, with waving flags and generals on prancing horses, — but war in its reality, in blood, in suffering, in death."

From the hospital the reader is led to the fourth bastion, and there sees the brave defenders of Sebastopol at work, dodging the bombs and bullets which come thick as hail and which strike and destroy the defenses and the defenders. Tolstoy stood at this most dangerous post for many months, every moment on the brink of eternity. What he saw and what he felt here was nearly always the human, and seldom the historic ; the canvases he paints are small, and he stints the color ; for he knows that only the superficial observer can see anything beautiful in war. Yet he, too, sees something of beauty, — not in march or countermarch, in cloud of smoke or flying bombs, but in the courage of the men, the bravery with which they do their duty, the fearlessness with which they meet death. He was very much respected and loved by the soldiers, for he was a faithful officer, a good comrade ; and in spite of the prevailing sadness could bring a trace of joy to the camp-fire. A captain who served with him thus describes him : " With his stories and his extemporized verses the Count cheered us all and made us forget the hardships of war. He was in the fullest sense of the word, the soul of the whole battery. When he was in our midst we did not realize how quickly the time passed ; when he was absent, all the comrades felt blue ; when he returned, he came like the prodigal son and confessed everything : how much he had lost at cards, how much he had drunk, and where and how he had spent his days and nights. His conscience troubled him and he acted as if he had

committed the greatest crimes; so that one had
to pity the poor fellow. As a man he was, in one
word, a queer fellow; and I must confess it, I did
not understand him; nevertheless, he was a splendid comrade, an honest soul, and he had a golden
heart. Whoever came really near to him had to
like and could not forget him." Indeed he was
a "good comrade," for it was he who startled
Russia by the story of its common soldiers' suffering and of their uncommon bravery. Not in bas-
tions, mines, and guns he discovers Russia's
strength, but in the spirit of its defenders.
"They cannot do this," he says, "because of
their love of a decoration, or because of fame, or
because they are driven to it — they suffer and
die because deep in the heart of every Russian
there is a great passion, a love for the Fatherland."

In Russia this story created a great sensation;
the empress wept over it, and the czar, Nicholas
I., gave order to have this young man kept in
view, and to remove him from his dangerous
post in the Fourth Battery. Tolstoy's heart and
mind were busy, for in the tumult of war he not
only wrote the first sketch, "Sebastopol in May,"

but he also continued to work upon his Caucasus material. After a blundering attack upon the enemy, in which the Russians were driven back with severe losses, a song was heard at the camp-fires ; a song in which in a caustic and humorous way Tolstoy described the encounter. The verse has no poetic merit : it is a mere jingle, and not really a good one, but I have translated it because it is his only effort in that direction with the exception of a few verses to his friend Fjett, which are of the same quality.

> How we, on the 4th of something,
> Carried by the Devil's prompting,
>   Went to rob the mountain.
>
> Baron Wrevsky,[1] full of drink,
> Tried to make Gorcakof[2] think
>   He must do his bidding.
>
> " Prince ! oh, follow my advice,
> If you think about it twice,
>   I will make report."
>
> Then the whole staff came together,
> With trailing sword and shining leather
>   And Major N. Bekok.

[1] General.
[2] Commander of Sebastopol.

TOLSTOY THE MAN

And the wise and brave Bekok
Sat there like a stupid block;
   Could not give an answer.

Long they talked and gave advice,
Topographs then drew plans nice,
   On a sheet of paper.

Very smooth and very fine
Looked on paper every line,
   Ravines they had forgotten.

Princes, Counts, to see the sport,
Rode as far as the big fort,
   With the topographs.

" Hey, Liprandi,[1] storm the height ! "
  He said, " Thank you " (in great fright),
   " I would rather not.

" With sense we cannot do this thing,
  Read [2] alone can vict'ry bring,
   Let me see him do it."

Read with courage goes along,
Soldiers follow with a song:
   " Hurrah ! to the bridge."

Martinau is vainly pleading,
" Wait for cavalry's relieving ; "
   " No, go storm the heights."

[1] General.
[2] General Read.

On they go with song and cheer,
But the horsemen are not here,
    Some one made a blunder.

Regiments went up the height;
Driven back in sorry plight,
    Companies returned.

Bravely there we held our place,
But of succor not a trace,
    Though we gave the signal.

With holy zeal the general prayed,
In safe and sacred spot he stayed
    Before the Virgin Mother.

Beaten worse than we can tell,
.   .   .   .
    Him who led us hither.

If the author's name had been mentioned, these verses would have cut short Tolstoy's military career, although he was not their originator. After the unsuccessful attack, the officers sat around the watch-fire talking it over, when some one suggested that each in turn compose a verse about the affair, which was so tragic and yet so ridiculous. The idea was taken up and created no end of fun, but the poem did not materialize.

The next day Tolstoy brought these verses, which were received with applause and soon were on every one's lips, making the lives of the generals mentioned in them far from comfortable. The verses are nowhere mentioned in Tolstoy's works, and to-day he laughs when they are spoken of, remembering them only as one of his boyish pranks, for which there was little opportunity during those months in which he was daily the companion of men "who were about to die." "Six months," he writes in his "Sebastopol in May," "have passed since the first bullet whistled across and demolished the earthworks thrown up by the enemy; since that time thousands of bombs, cannon-balls, and bullets have flown from the fort to the earthworks, and from the earthworks to the fort; the death angel has hovered over them unceasingly, . . . and the question which statesmen could not answer has not yet found its solution through powder and shot."

Still the band plays on the boulevard as in time of peace, while officers, gayly dressed women and children walk about with a holiday air. Tolstoy makes us acquainted with Captain Michailof, who goes for the thirteenth time to the battery, is depressed by the unlucky number, and full of apprehension. He has gone voluntarily to this dangerous post, and in him struggle bravery and fear, humility and pride, the desire to live and the horror of death. We follow, too, another officer, Kalugin, who seeks honor, glory, and shelter. Unsurpassed in deep and quiet tragedy is the death of Praskuchin, an officer who follows Michailof to the most dangerous place on the battery, and there is struck by an exploding bomb. "The second which passed between the lighting of the bomb and its explosion seemed an hour, and sharp, short, and conflicting are the thoughts which pass through his mind." "Perhaps it will not explode at all," he says to himself, when through his shut eyelids there penetrates a red flame, and with a dreadful crash something heavy strikes his breast. "Thank God, I am only wounded," was his first thought, and he wanted to feel his breast, but his hands seemed to be chained, and a peculiar weight pressed his head. He counts, "one, two, three soldiers, and there is an officer with his mantle thrown back. Lightning flames in his eyes, and he wonders with what they are shooting, mortars or guns.

It must be guns. Again they are shooting, and again there are soldiers, five, six, seven, and they all pass by. Suddenly the fear rose in him that they might crush him. He wished to call out that he was wounded, but his mouth was so dry that his tongue clove to his gums, and a dreadful thirst tortured him. He felt his breast wet; it reminded him of water, and he would have liked to drink that from which came the sensation. He summoned all his strength and tried to call out : 'Lift me up;' but instead of that he only groaned, which was terrible for him to hear. Then little red flames danced before his eyes, and he felt as if soldiers laid stones upon him, and they took his breath more and more; he attempted to push the stones away, he stretched himself, and already he saw nothing, felt nothing, thought nothing; — a burst shell had struck him in the breast, and he was killed immediately."

In spite of dreadful torture, and the fear of death in its many forms which Tolstoy saw and described, he was for a moment elated by the prevailing patriotic spirit, and says : " The siege of Sebastopol, in which the Russian nation was such a hero, will leave its trace upon Russia," but in the same breath he wonders "whether war is not a mistake, in which the nations are entangled without cause." The people do not hate each other; watch them during that time when the "white flag of truce waves over the blossoming valley which is covered by corpses." Many thousands of people push against one another there; smilingly they talk to each other; two men who meet converse together in a most peaceful way: "Are you from the staff?" "No; I am from the Sixth Infantry." "Where did you buy this?" "At Balaklava." "It is pretty," says the one officer. "If you will take it as a memento of our meeting, you are welcome to it;" and the polite Frenchman hands the cigarette-case to the receptive Russian, who in turn gives him his own. They are pleased by this episode, and all who see it smile. Thus the officers talk one to the other, and the common soldiers meet their comrades with still less ceremony. "Tabak bung," says the soldier with the red shirt; and the bystanders laugh. "Oui; bun tabak Turc and Russ tabak bun?" answers the Frenchman. "Russ bun," says the soldier with the red shirt;

TOLSTOY'S HOME IN MOSCOW

and all around them laugh so heartily that they nearly roll on the ground. "France not bun, bunshur, mussyo," continues the soldier, exhausting his stock of the foreign tongue, and good-naturedly hitting the Frenchman in the stomach. Thus they continue to laugh together, men who poured gunshot at one another an hour ago, and who will do the same thing again as soon as the signal is given. They chat and laugh, indifferent to the tremendous carnage which they have strewn about them, and unconscious of the great wrong perpetrated by them and against them.

Here Tolstoy strikes the first strong note of that terrible indictment against war, which was to make of him the most famous peace apostle of our times. "And these Christians," he says, "who confess the same Christian law of love and self-sacrifice, do not fall repentingly upon their knees at the sight of what they have done. The white flags are drawn in, anew the instruments of death and suffering whistle their horrible tune, and one hears sighs and curses." Again he leads us to "Sebastopol in May," and still more fearful are the pictures unrolled. The Russians are exhausted but not discouraged, and we meet the

same soldier, brave and obedient, who has in him
more virtues than the officers know or care to know,
and who goes to his death uncomplainingly. We
follow two brothers, one of them fresh from St.
Petersburg, where he "was ashamed to remain
when others die for the Fatherland." He finds his
company on the Malachof heights, and his brother
takes leave of him for the last time. That day ends
the siege, and brings Sebastopol's doom. The older
brother receives his death wound, and as the chap-
lain hands him the cross, he asks : "Have we beaten
the French ?" and the man of comfort, who does
not wish to pain the dying man, answers : "The
victory is ours." At the last moment the soldier
thinks of his younger brother, wishing him to share
his fate, and his desire is fulfilled ; for the young
boy's flesh is crushed underneath the feet of the
advancing French.

Sebastopol is to be evacuated, the remaining
forts are blown up, and slowly the columns move
into the impenetrable darkness. The soldiers leave
the place with mingled feelings of shame, regret,
and gratitude that their lives were spared ; but
as each man passes over the bridge which leads
to safety, he crosses himself and then shakes his

fist at the victorious foe. Tolstoy also left the battlefield, and after acting for a time as an imperial courier, he took his leave of the army, having seen three years of arduous service. It was the most important period of his life; it brought latent thoughts to maturity, it increased his love for the common man, and his horror of war. It gave him a chance to see humanity at its best and at its worst; he had helped many a man to die, and that gave him an increased desire to live. He seemed to have had a glimpse of the most secret recesses of men's hearts, and in learning to know others, he learned to know himself. He had not as yet a philosophy of life, but he was feeling after it. In the chaos of war he came near the true source of peace; laurels, too, he gained, upon a field on which the sword had been supplanted by the pen, which henceforth was to be his only weapon.

CHAPTER VI

RUSSIA was in the stage of fermentation. The unfortunate policy of Nicholas had brought untold ruin upon all classes, which sullenly expressed their discontent, while demanding and expecting relief. Thirty-three million people, the bone and sinew of Russia, its patient, toiling peasants, were the property of the aristocrats, who with their increased burdens, pressed more heavily upon the already crushed mujik. During the disastrous Crimean war the peasants had been called from their far-off villages to be drilled and made ready for the defense of their country; their drill-masters were pensioned officers, students, artists, and officials; all of them discontented. Their spirit quickly communicated itself to the peasantry, which for the first time heard a complaint that harmonized with its own repressed feelings.

Alexander II., whose humane policy will always remain like the touch of a sunburst upon a storm-

laden sky, permitted in the public press the discussion of existing wrongs in order to pacify the
discontented, as well as to get a perspective for
his own plan of action. In the capital on the Neva
had gathered Russia's struggling authors, who had
been caught in the prevailing upward pressure, and
were ready to write the wrongs of the people
and to dream about the unknown and better things
before them. A journal founded by Puschkin, and
now edited by Panaieff and Nekrassoff, gave them
the battlefield on which they bravely struggled
against Eastern conservatism, and where they
broke many a lance for Western culture. To us,
the names of Turgenieff and Dostoyefsky, who
were the leaders of the movement, are warrants
of its literary standard ; and that Tolstoy was
immediately received into this circle as an equal
shows to what heights he had risen while alternately wielding the sword and the pen. He came
to St. Petersburg from the deprivations of a besieged city, and drew in with deep breath all that it
could yield him. He soon made the acquaintance
of Turgenieff, who was then at the height of his
literary fame and known beyond the boundaries
of his own country ; not a trace of jealousy was

visible in him, although he saw in Tolstoy a rising literary star, an equal and a brother, whom he received into his home most cordially, although he was not a comfortable guest. He came home whenever he pleased, which was always long after midnight, sleeping until noon, and beyond it; and inasmuch as he occupied the parlor of his host, who believed in " early to bed and early to rise," the latter was not a little incommoded.

The poet Schenshin, known by the pseudonym "Fjett," and who remained in unbroken friendship with Tolstoy, saw him here for the first time. Tolstoy was still in bed when he arrived, although the morning was far advanced; and when "Fjett" expressed his surprise, Turgenieff said : " He does that all the time; he has come back from Sebastopol and his battery, and he is beside himself. Cards, gypsies, and drinking, the whole night, and then he sleeps like a corpse till afternoon. At first I tried to hold him back, but now I have given it up."

Tolstoy's excessive nature could not be held in check; he sinned every day like the most depraved mujik, but repented as magnificently as King David. All that he had condemned, and was to condemn still more severely, he tasted through and through, and found pleasure in it. His perfectly open nature, which tempted him to tell everybody just what he thought and as he thought it, led him into severe conflicts with his colleagues, and especially with Turgenieff, who was a perfect idealist in his early years and full of mannerisms, which seemed to Tolstoy insincerities. Theirs were two opposite natures, both of them too strong and individualistic to cling to each other. They were constantly quarreling like two spoiled boys, agreeing best when Turgenieff was in Paris, and Tolstoy in Moscow or Yasnaya Polyana. How trivial these quarrels were, their common friend "Fjett" reports after witnessing the following in Nekrassoff's home, where both of them were visitors. "Turgenieff walked up and down the room with gigantic steps, piteously groaning, holding his throat with both hands, and whispering with the eyes of a dying gazelle : 'I am done for, I have bronchitis.' Tolstoy, like an angry bear, said roughly, 'Bronchitis is a disease of the imagination.' Nekrassoff's heart sank into his boots, for he is the editor of the 'Journal,' of which these two are the main pillars, and he is eager to avoid a rupture ; he would like to take Turgenieff's part, but fears to offend Tolstoy, who is lying, angry, on the sofa. Turgenieff, with his hands in his pockets and his coat-tails swinging, walks up and down the three rooms. Everybody is excited and nobody knows what to do. Expecting a catastrophe, I step to the sofa and say : ' My dearest Tolstoy, don't be excited. You do not know how he values you and how he loves you.' ' I cannot permit him,' replies Tolstoy, with expanded nostrils, ' to do anything to spite me ; now he walks purposely up and down in front of me, and turns his democratic shin-bones hither and thither.' "

Their whole early acquaintance is spoiled by such trivialities, which are unfortunately connected with the lives of great people, and which spring sometimes from their overwrought nerves, but more often from the fact that many an unripened genius thinks incivility the sign of budding strength and greatness. A year after this quarrel, Turgenieff writes Tolstoy from Paris, " Our acquaintance was formed under wrong conditions ; when we meet again it will be easier and better." But afterwards he writes: "A strong friendship between us is impossible, for we are formed of different clay."

Tolstoy's self-appreciation, heightened by the self-conscious atmosphere which prevailed in his literary circle, and by the praise which was showered upon him, destroyed all his reserve, and made him the storm-center of every company. He was used to dealing roughly and honestly with himself, and he thought that he could do it with others. At one of these gatherings he called out excitedly, "I cannot admit that your words express your convictions. I stand here with my sword or dagger, and I say: 'So long as I live, nobody shall pass this threshold;' that is conviction, but you try to hide from one another your real thoughts, and you call that conviction." Turgenieff, for whom this sally was intended, cried out angrily, "Get out! your banner does not wave here." The trouble was that most of the men who composed this circle were dreamers who had ideals, but could not coin them into words, and much less into deeds, while Tolstoy was as eager for action then as he was on the Fourth Battery face to face with the enemy.

He had in him that elementary force which brooks no opposition, which has no sense of the common and the commonplace, and no use for them ; which disregards all traditions, breaks abruptly from the past, and takes hold of the present as if it were the first day of creation. Out of such a mood came his unfortunate criticisms of Shakespeare and his admirers, of Goethe and his Faust, and of Herzen the Russian author, whose name was then upon everybody's lips. Among men of lesser strength his words carried conviction, while among his equals and friends they created discords and quarrels, and broke binding ties, consequences which he did not care to avoid, at the expense of what he considered "truth." He also believed that one must have a definite philosophy of life, and that one must aim for moral perfection in himself and others, theories which were not considered necessary by his friends, among whom art was a great goddess, and "art for art's sake" a formula not yet expressed but felt, and one which Tolstoy was always ready to combat. What contributed not a little to his irritability was that he fancied himself ill, for consumption was in his family, his best beloved brother being then in its first stages. But more perhaps than anything else his disquiet grew from the fact that he did not live up to his ideals. Each day with him was a struggle for moral perfection, and each day saw his defeat. Such physical, mental, and spiritual unrest does not make a man a good companion, although in spite of it, the artist continued to grow, and perhaps because of it, his creative power became stronger and stronger.

He wrote during this time another fragment of the never-completed biographical story, " Youth," " The Notebook of a Scorekeeper," " The Two Hussars," " The Blizzard," and " Albert." " The Notebook of a Scorekeeper " is one of the keenest criticisms which he has written, of the life around him : aside from its artistic merit, it ought to be of the greatest importance as a tract against the passion of gambling. Just as mercilessly as he had pictured war, with its useless and terrible sacrifice of life, he now describes the struggle with that passion which has ruined such large fortunes, so much character, and so many lives. Delicately yet fearlessly and plainly he describes Nechludoff's first step to-

ward moral ruin; and although it all happened
in St. Petersburg, we recognize in his surroundings the "men of the world" who are everywhere the same, eager to lead others astray, and
doing it without the slightest twinge of conscience. On the contrary, they are proud of the
fact that they have guided an innocent youth to
the path which they call the way of life, but
which is the way of death. "You may laugh
about it," says Nechludoff blushingly, "Prince, I
shall never forgive you or myself." "Don't cry,"
says the prince jokingly, "we shall ride home."
"I don't want to ride anywhere. Oh! what have
I done?" Thus he sighed, yet did not move
away from the billiard-table. "He had been as
innocent as a young girl." This same circle which
had prided itself upon destroying his innocence
also enticed him to ruin his fortune. Pitiable are
those steps downward, and we follow him trem-
blingly. He has gambled away all he had; he is
possessed by the demon; he borrows money, the
money of the poor scorekeeper; he is wanted
less and less as his fortune is reduced, and finally
the keeper of the house refuses openly to trust
him longer. Weighed down by the shame, struck

Drawn by L. Pasternak

FROM THE STATION TO YASNAYA POLYANA

in the vital part of his sensitive soul, he sends the scorekeeper out of the room and kills himself.

That this was written out of Tolstoy's own experience we know, and that he was near committing suicide is admitted by him; that he was chastising himself and trying to cure himself of the evil which possessed him are plainly seen. The story is not less tragic and awful than any of his war stories, and the color is as gray and dark as that which hung over Sebastopol. He takes all the romance out of the social vices, just as he blurred all the bright colors in our conception of war.

With less artistic skill but not less forcibly, he wrote the story of "The Two Hussars," in which he puts opposite each other father and son; one of them a man of the old school, who loves "wine, women, and song," an unscrupulous Don Juan, and his son, who comes to the scene of his father's adventures, with high ideals of life, with an abhorrence of war, and great love for the simple domestic life. These are the two points upon which Tolstoy is to enlarge more and more in his work and in his life, and which here serve only as preliminary sketches.

In his simple but powerful story " The Blizzard," it is as if an artist had unexpectedly turned from the painting of figures to that of landscapes, for Tolstoy suddenly becomes descriptive, and silences all his critics who still claim that he has no feeling for nature. He tells of his journey from one post-station to another, on a stormy winter's night; of the increasing darkness, the howling wind, the driving snow, the long wandering through the trackless night, and the impressions made upon him by the illimitable space. Clearly, as if painted upon canvas by the best artist, the picture remains before our eyes, and we wander with him like that lost speck which he was, upon the snowy desert. This feeling for nature is one of Tolstoy's artistic qualities which he purposely suppressed, and only once more does it appear in all its fullness : that is in the forty-third chapter of "War and Peace," which Turgenieff called " the finest descriptive scene in European literature." Nearing the form of a novel, and yet with scarcely any plot, is the next story, "Albert," which Tolstoy began at this time, and finished during his stay abroad. The hero of the story is a German mu-

sician, the one whom Tolstoy dragged with him
to Yasnaya Polyana, and whom he tried to save
for himself and his art. To Tolstoy he is that not
very uncommon type of the musician, who has
great talent but not much character. In him the
vital fiber remained undeveloped, and in educating
the artist, the man was lost. Without and within
he is neglected, — bow-legged, a narrow, bent
back, long disheveled hair, his thin white neck
encircled by a cravat which looks like a rope,
while from his sleeves the dirty shirt protrudes
itself. Delesoff (Tolstoy) found him in a dubious
locality, where he delighted the mixed company
by his magnificent playing. Delesoff is attracted
to him, takes him home, and is anxious to build
up in him his destroyed manhood; but his benevo-
lence is a torture to the musician, to whom the
well-ordered life and the comfort of the home
seem a penalty rather than a benefaction. He
is detained by force for three days, but finally
escapes his rescuer, and is found frozen to death
at the entrance to the ball-room. In reality,
the musician remained longer with Tolstoy, and
helped to develop his musical talent, which is not
inconsiderable. It is in this story that Tolstoy

first hints at his condemnation of art, which often makes itself both one's creator and destroyer.

"The Cossacks," mentioned in a previous chapter, is one of five stories written during this period by Tolstoy, which increased his fame, and caused the gentle and forgiving Turgenieff to write from Paris: "When this wine is clarified it will be a drink worthy of the gods;" and to Tolstoy he wrote at the same time: "If you do not swerve from your purpose (and there is no reason that you should) you will do great things." Yet his literary reputation satisfied him as little as his military laurels, and his desire to come in touch with the forward movement of the world led him in 1857 to Europe, and directly to Paris, the Mecca of Russian intelligence.

CHAPTER VII

As far as the Neva is from the Seine, so far does
the spirit of the Slav seem from that of the
Latin. Heavy, sedate, impassive, he presents a
complete contrast to the lithe, passionate, and
graceful Frenchman, to whom nevertheless he
feels himself drawn, and with whom he is closely
allied whether their respective countries are at
peace or not. It may be that Paris grew to be
the Mecca of the Russians only in that sense in
which it has been that of the whole intellectual
and pleasure-loving world ; or the Russians may
have been drawn there by finding in it the very
things which their own nation and country
lacked, or what seems more likely still, they were
attracted to each other by a real kinship of
spirit which does not appear to the superficial
observer. The Germany which lies between
these two countries, with its deep intellectual-
ity, its love of law and order, its correctness and

its brusqueness, never had a great attraction for the Russian, who usually passed through it without noticing it, and without knowing or caring to know it. Tolstoy also passed through it quickly, and yet his sharp, discerning eyes noticed, as soon as he crossed the Russian border, that he was in a country full of "courage and vigor;" that each patch of soil showed cultivation, and that it was a land worth knowing better. He promised himself a prolonged visit on his return trip, and hurried on to Paris, where he arrived early in February, 1857.

In Tolstoy's notebook nothing is found which shows what effect Paris had upon him, and he seldom speaks of his experiences abroad, nor is the influence visible in any of his works. He saw in Paris the same human beings whom he had seen in St. Petersburg, with the same sorrows and cares, the same passions and desires; and although he found more culture, he did not find more virtue. If the architecture of its churches and palaces was different, and customs and habits unlike those at home, love and hate, happiness and misery, were the same. Above all, he found that the spirit which permeated

French society was identical with that in Russia, having the same faults and the same virtues. The happy-go-lucky, easy-going, pleasure-loving crowd which surged up and down the Nevsky Prospect, he saw also on the Parisian boulevards. In Paris, to be sure, the crowd flaunted its luxuries more gracefully, and it drank absinthe instead of vodka ; but it came on the scene at just about the same hour, and turned night into day in just about the same way. It was the same chess-board, only on one side there were more pawns and on the other side more kings, while on both sides the game of life was played carelessly ; but when one lost it said "nytshevo," and the other perhaps sought the quickest way to the morgue. Tolstoy was not caught in the Parisian whirl, and, if he indulged in any of its pleasures, he did not grow so dizzy that he could not still see the only thing to him worth seeing, — the individual human being. He attended the lectures in the Sorbonne, rode in an omnibus up and down the boulevards, walked through the narrow streets where the toilers lived, went to the prisons, and attended the execution of a criminal. This single death made more impression upon him than the life of the gay crowd upon the streets, and his whole nature revolted against so cruel and inexcusable an act. He still hears how the head rolled into the wooden casket, and how the headless body followed it; still sees the flowing blood, the inquisitive throng, and all the gruesome surroundings of this scene, which made him rebel against a civilization which not only allowed but took satisfaction in it.

In Paris he again met Turgenieff (who had grown fond of France and could scarcely exist in his own country), Nekrassoff, who was also visiting there, and many other lesser lights who had come for inspiration. They found Tolstoy a better companion than he had been in St. Petersburg, which was probably due to the fact that he was living a more regular life, and that he indulged in no excesses; consequently his nerves were steadier, and he talked less and worked more. During his stay in Paris he lived in one of those international pensions in which it abounds, and of which he says: "There were twenty of us of different nationalities, callings, and characteristics; but under the influence of French sociability we gathered around the table

as if we were a pleasure party. From one end
to the other the jests and jokes were passed,
often in mutilated languages. Everybody talked,
without a care as to how his words would be
received : we had our philosopher, our fighting
rooster, our poet, our fool, and they belonged to
all of us. After the meal we pushed the table
aside and danced on the dusty carpet, in time and
tune or out of them, until late in the evening.
Perhaps we flirted a little bit : we were not
always very sensible or reverent people, nevertheless we were human beings. There were the
Spanish countess with her romantic adventures,
the American doctor who had access to the Tui-
leries, the young tragedian with his long hair,
the pianist who herself said that she had composed the finest polka in the world, and the unfortunate, beautiful widow with her three rings
on each finger. We associated one with the other
in a somewhat superficial but altogether delight-
ful fashion, and took away with us passing or
deeper memories of one another."

In April and May of the same year, Tolstoy
was in Italy ; but, strange to say, he seemed to be
unimpressed by it. The ecstasies with which

every one speaks of its blue skies and matchless seas found in him no echo; and he passed
through the Eternal City, through Florence and
Venice, as if he had been both deaf and blind.
Only in conversation with friends who have traveled does he here and there drop a few words;
but they add nothing to our knowledge of his
impressions, for they are often only trivial anecdotes and nothing more. In reality, he walked
through Italy like an iconoclastic Puritan; so full
of thoughts of man's sins and man's sufferings
that hardly a ray of its matchless beauty penetrated those sharp, half-closed eyes, shaded by a
knitted brow. In Italy too many beggars hung
at his heels for him to take any pleasure in visiting palaces; he saw too much ignorance and
superstition to believe in the elevating influences
of that art by which its museums and galleries
were crowded; and, above all, Italy spoke only of
the past, and in that Tolstoy had little interest.
He was never a hero-worshiper, did not care for
tombs or monuments, and his guides found him
a skeptical, an irreverent, and unwilling victim.
Although he had not then formulated a theory
of art, he had given the subject much thought;

and the classic nudeness was to him not the less nude simply because it was classic. And just because he had a strong and sensuous nature he felt keenly its influence and often knew himself too debased to express himself exaltedly.

In Switzerland, where nature was not spoiled by the artifices of men, his artistic soul was touched ; and he quivers from emotion at the sight of it. He writes in his " Luzerne " : " As I went up to my room and opened my window toward the lake, I was literally dazed and overwhelmed in the first moments by the beauty of the water, the mountains, and the sky. I felt an unrest, a desire in some way to give expression to the overflowing emotions which were suddenly filling my soul. . . . But neither on the lake, on the mountains, nor in the sky was there one straight line visible, or one definite color, or yet one quiet point; everywhere there were motion, irregularity, arbitrariness, endless variety of light and shade, but also in everything the quiet, the softness, the harmony, the necessity of the beautiful." At the sight of what man had done, he felt here just what Ruskin felt ; nor does he condemn less severely and sarcastically. "And here, in the midst of this indefinite, confused, and wild beauty, there stared at me from under my windows, stupid and foolish, the white line of the boulevard, the linden-trees with their supports, the green benches, poor miserable works of human hands, which did not disappear in the surrounding loveliness, like the distant villas and ruins, but which coarsely opposed it."

He was able, however, to find a spot where he did not see the straight English tourist among the straight linden-trees, on that horribly straight boulevard, and where he indulged "in that incomplete but therefore sweeter pleasure which one feels when one beholds the beauty of nature all alone." He does not revel very long in this solitary ecstasy, for he comes in touch with a poor dwarfed musician who plays on his guitar and sings the songs of the mountains, before a hundred admiring guests of the hotel, and afterwards is sent away without the smallest reward for his work. Tolstoy pityingly follows the man, talks to him, and returns with him to the elegant hotel in which he played. He takes him to the dining-salon, and is refused admittance because of his companion; but in spite of opposition he enters with him, and a well-fed, well-dressed Englishman immediately leaves his table and complains because of the intrusion.

This simple incident left a powerful impression on Tolstoy and furnishes the text for his first attack upon society, " Luzerne." It is severe and sarcastic, yet so artistically done and so deeply felt that it escapes classification among his sociological tracts. " That is the strange fate of poetry," he says, walking restlessly under those straight linden-trees ; " everybody loves it and desires it, but nobody acknowledges its power. Ask all the guests of the ' Schweitzerhof ' what is the highest gift of Earth, and all, or ninety-nine out of one hundred, will answer : ' The best gift of Earth is money.' And yet they have all left their comfortable homes in the far corners of the world, for . . . the poetry which they find in these mountains ; that same poetry of which they talk sarcastically and which they admit is good for children and young girls." He cannot cut himself loose from the thought that no man gave anything to the musician, to whom they all listened, and in whose music they found pleasure. Emphatically and angrily he writes: "On the seventh of July, 1857, in Luzerne, at the hotel Schweitzerhof, in which the richest tourists live, a poor wandering musician played on his guitar and sang for half an hour. About a hundred people listened to him; but although the singer asked them three times for a gift, not one of them gave him the smallest sum, and most of them laughed at him."

To Tolstoy this is important enough to be written by the chronicler with a fiery pen on the page of history; it is more important and of deeper significance than the things we read of in our newspapers and histories.

"That the English have killed thousands of Chinese because they do not buy for cash, that the French have again killed a thousand natives in Africa simply because the grain grows abundantly and because an uninterrupted war is good for the development of the army, that the Turkish consul in Naples must not be a Jew, that the Emperor Napoleon is taking a walk in Plombières and has assured his people in black and white that he ascends the throne only to please them, — all these things are empty words

which express well-known facts or which are
only meant to hide their real meaning : — but
that which happened in Luzerne on the seventh
of July, seems to me entirely new and remarkable, and has no bearing upon what we call the
bad traits of human nature ; it is a definite
phase of our social development. That is a fact,
not for the history of human actions, but for
the history of progress and civilization."

His righteous indignation at a wrong against
one human being seems almost ridiculous ; but it
has always been and has remained his habit to see
in the one wronged man the wronged human
race ; and no less clearly to see in the attitude of
the mass the one dominating thought, the whole
attitude, of modern civilization. And as there in
Luzerne gathered its best results, the incident
of the musician proved to him that culture has
destroyed in man his simple, natural, and original
feeling toward others. He reasoned that in no
village in Russia would this have been possible.
The mujik is uneducated, but he knows that he
is in some way responsible for his brother ;
he is coarse in conversation, but he has that fine
feeling for others which expresses itself in his

conduct toward all the unfortunate. He is sometimes brutal, but never so brutal that he would turn away a man who had given him pleasure without recompensing him for it.

Here among cultured people Tolstoy does not find any of these qualities; consequently he thinks that civilization has destroyed them and that it is in some way to blame. Less pedantic and arbitrary than his accusation and reasoning is his solution of all the problems : —

"One, only one infallible guide have we : that Spirit which embraces us all, which permeates each individual, and which has put into all of us the desire to seek the good; the same Spirit which works in the tree that it may grow toward the sun, which operates in the flower that it may scatter seed in the autumn, and which dwells in us unconsciously that we may be drawn toward one another." Yet this somewhat indefinite solution was not altogether satisfactory; he felt that it was "vague phrase," and it left him just as undecided as before. He was simply drifting with the current, "like a man sitting in a boat driven by the wind and waves, who might be asked : 'Where are you going?' and who could not answer : 'I am going there or there.' "

Neither his European visit nor his touch with European scholars brought rest to his ever-questioning soul; and although he was to come to them again and again, and was to "ask and seek and knock" at strange doors, he already felt that the answer was not written in any philosophy ; but that it has been worked out in "The One Life," after which he, and every individual, with much sacrifice and labor, must pattern.

CHAPTER VIII

DURING the winter of 1857 Tolstoy was again in Moscow, and in spite of his repeated "preachments" against civilization he indulged himself in those aspects of it which are simply refined barbarities, and of which each generation inherits its full measure. Of those phases of modern progress Russia had its share even before it was civilized ; and the man who said, "Let us eat and drink and be merry, for to-morrow we die," now has numerous descendants in its villages and cities. Temptation has here a peculiar quality ; for the busiest brain soon succumbs to the prevailing spirit of idleness, while the most virtuous man has at least his recurring temptations ; and Tolstoy became a genuine Muscovitic aristocrat before he was aware of it. He sinned under protest, to be sure ; but that did not make the champagne less intoxicating, the cards less dangerous to his fortune, or the black-eyed gypsy maidens less ruinous to his morals. This life put him simply on a level with other young men of his time and station; for at this stage of his development he had only the inclination but not the courage to be odd.

These rough pleasures, this sowing of his "wild oats," did not close a single door against him, and caused less comment than if he had abstained from them. Nor did he cease taking full delight in higher pleasures; for he was a constant guest in the home of his friend "Fyett," where an artistic and musical housewife gathered around her the intelligence of Moscow, and where many a new symphony and many a new song had their first interpretation, which caused endless debate. Tolstoy not only listened intelligently to music, but was a fine performer, being especially sought after to play accompaniments; for he was a master in that difficult and thankless art. Sometimes he skipped these musical "jours"; particularly when he knew that some tedious guests were to be present, or when he suspected his friend "Fyett" of intending to practice on the company his poems or translations of Shakespeare.

At this time Tolstoy had, in common with all the idle and noble youth of his acquaintance, a hobby imported from the West; and that was gymnastics. The inactive young men of Moscow, who found no greater pleasure than to be whirled along, sitting behind fast horses, had suddenly become active, and a large club-house was opened in which they practiced their new accomplishment. Tolstoy entered into this latest fashion with all the ardor of his strong physical nature, and every day at noon could be found here "dressed in pink tights, hanging by his toes on the trapeze, his bushy hair over his face." When he had exhausted himself here, he walked up and down the Tverskaya, the loafing-place of Moscow's gilded youth: he was always dressed in the height of fashion, his hat tilted, and a cane twirling between his fingers, — the very picture of a dandy.

Suddenly he disappeared from Moscow, and as suddenly appeared in Paris, from where he went to Dijon and again began to gather his scattered strength to write his sketch, "Albert," the story of the unfortunate musician, to which reference has already been made.

TOLSTOY THE MAN

By Christmas he is again in Yasnaya Polyana, and ends a rather idle and unprofitable year, only to begin another one in the same way in the same place. In the winter he hunted, and came near losing his life at a bear-chase to which a friend had invited him and "Fyett," who relates the incident graphically: "Tolstoy stood nearly up to his waist in the snow, when a powerful bear appeared and went straight at him in a decidedly unneighborly fashion. Tolstoy aimed and fired, but failed; and in the smoke he saw the towering body of the animal ready to throw itself upon him. He shot again; this time the bullet entered the animal's mouth, but was deflected by the teeth. Tolstoy did not have time to grasp another gun, nor could he jump out of the way; he felt a sudden stroke and fell backward on the snow; but the bear's aim was as bad as his own. It sprang too far, and as it returned, ready to devour the frightened hunter, he had presence of mind enough to push his big fur cap into its jaws and for the moment avert a renewed attack, until one of the foresters could come to his aid and drive away the monster." Tolstoy was found to be badly bitten and bleeding; but the first thing he said was, "What will Fyett think about it?"

During that year he lived in close intimacy with this poet, whom he called his "little darling," and whom he loved for his gifts as a poet and as a man. This was the year in which Tolstoy began to be so remarkably interested in farm labor; and his brother describes how he saw him walking behind the plow just like a peasant. Tolstoy himself narrates their conversation about it, in "Anna Karénina," where a great deal of his inner and outer life is portrayed. With marvelous energy he gives himself to the tilling of the soil, yet reserves enough leisure to enjoy all the beauties of the changing seasons; drinking them all in, in strong draughts. "What a marvelous day it has been," he writes of the Pentecostal holyday; "what a beautiful church service; the fading blossoms of the redbud, the gray hair of the peasants, their bright red coats, and the glowing, burning sun!" He testifies to his close touch with nature during this period, by writing the last part of "The Three Deaths," in which he graphically describes the death of the tree. He did not neglect his

COUNTESS TOLSTOY

gymnastic exercises, but practiced faithfully, to
the great amusement of the peasants and the
chagrin of his brother Nicolai, who writes :
" Lyoftschik (a pet name) wants to do everything, and everything at once, and he does
not want to give up his gymnastics. Near
the window of his workroom is the apparatus.
Of course he does as he pleases, and does n't
care what others say about it ; but the village
elder finds it rather queer, and says : ' I come to
the master for orders, but he is dressed in a red
jacket, and, with one knee over a pole and his
head downward, is swinging himself. His hair
hangs down and waves in all directions, the
blood has rushed to his face, and one does not
know whether just to gaze at him or to ask for
one's orders.' "

The year 1859 was spent in Moscow, with
long intervals at Yasnaya Polyana, and one or
two visits to St. Petersburg. During this year
Tolstoy wrote his story, " Family Happiness,"
and finished that remarkable sketch already re-
ferred to, " Three Deaths." The story, " Family
Happiness," is charming ; an adjective which
does not fit many of his best and strongest

works. A seventeen-year-old girl, Mascha, an orphan, lives alone with her governess and younger sister on their estate, and falls in love with the first man who comes into her awakened woman's soul; that man being Sergei Michaelovitsch, her neighbor and guardian. The affection which springs in the heart of each is ardent and sweet, and its awakening is pictured with the touch of a man who has the highest conception of human love. Sergei is nineteen years older than Mascha, and is much in doubt whether he ought to link the life of so young a girl to his; but love, which is stronger than doubt, conquers, and they marry and live happily at his country place.

The happiness which Tolstoy here pictures is the longing of his own love-hungry heart. "A quiet if lonely life, far away from the city yet near enough to men, with the possibility of being of service to such as are unused to kindness, and whom it is easy to befriend; to do the kind of work which one believes to be useful. Then recreation, nature, books, music, love for a congenial soul; that is my happiness, and I cannot imagine anything higher or better." Yet the happiness of which the hero of the story dreams is not the happiness for which his wife longs; she grows restless and sighs for the life of the city. They move to the capital, she is caught in the whirl of its pleasures, and does not wish to return to the country with her husband; so, in spite of their two children, a break occurs, and he goes home alone. She does not realize her position or how others may regard it, until an Italian count tries to make love to her. Then she returns to her husband; but the happiness which they now find lacks the fire and the romance of the love which was lost, although it grows strong and pure in their common devotion to their children.

This story is important because the author is trying to formulate a theory of marriage, and a happiness in married life which is not based upon the carnal or what men call the romantic, but upon something purer, deeper, and better. As if to foreshadow his own coming experience, he wrote the story, "Three Deaths." The unwilling and harrowing death of the rich woman who clings to every fiber of life until the last moment, is contrasted with the death of the old, worn-out peasant, whose life indeed was "labor and sorrow," but who glides quietly into the unknown, without fear. Crude, rough, and rude are his surroundings, yet no lying phrase reaches his ears, which are soon to be closed to all human sound. He gives his boots, his only treasure, to the boy who watches by him, and asks in return some memorial upon his grave, — a stone or a wooden cross. He dies almost as quietly as the tree which is cut down by the boy, and out of which he will make the cross for the peasant's grave.

These two stories dealt with problems which had not yet come into Tolstoy's life for solution, but which were coming nearer to him every moment. His favorite brother, Nikolai, was showing strong symptoms of consumption ; so it was decided to send him abroad, his brother Sergei and his sister Maria accompanying him. Soden, in Germany, was chosen by the physicians as the proper place in which to effect a cure, and inasmuch as Turgenieff was also there, the decision was quickly made and carried out. Turgenieff was exceedingly fond of Nikolai, whom he called "The Old Sage," and of whom he said after his death, " he was a splendid man ; smart, humble, and kindly affectionate." After his brother's departure Tolstoy felt very much depressed. The business of carrying on his estate grew burdensome, anxiety for his brother, from whom he had not heard since his arrival abroad, oppressed him; so, to relieve himself and be near his brother and of service to his sister, he decided to go to them, and wrote to his friend "Fyett" to that effect.

His journey this time was by way of St. Petersburg and the sea. He reached Stettin on the fifth of July, leaving immediately for Berlin, where he arrived with a torturing toothache which spoiled for him the first few days of his stay there. Germany could not fail to be interesting to Tolstoy; for it was not only the land of the modern philosopher but also the country in which the social question was taken from the revolutionary arena into the peaceful schoolroom to find itself interpreted in law and life. Berlin was beginning to be the great intellectual and political center, and already had in it those elements which have since made it one of the most beautiful and best governed cities in Europe. While Tolstoy felt everywhere the severity of law, he also felt the strong undercurrent of love which was then drawing men together and creating that class consciousness which made of the laborer's cap a crown, and of Social Democracy a religion.

He heard a number of popular lectures upon sociological subjects, attended sessions of the Worker's Union, and listened to a few lectures at the university which revealed to him the quality of the German pedagogic pabulum. What interested him most was the public-school system; and he went purposely to Leipsic to have a glimpse of its schools, which were considered the best in the country.

From Berlin he went to Dresden, where he visited Berthold Auerbach, whose stories he had read, and to whom he felt himself greatly drawn. Auerbach was as much the revealer of the German peasant as Tolstoy was of the Russian, although they stood in different relation to their subjects. Auerbach contrasted the straightforwardness and honesty of village life with the corruptness and complexity of the life of the city, and tried to liberate the peasant from the slavery of the new civilization which was being pressed upon him, much against his will. The simplicity of Auerbach's narrative, the educational quality by which his work is permeated, the purity and nobility of his life, attracted Tolstoy, and the few days that they spent together in Dresden were memorable to both of them.

Tolstoy next went to Kissingen, where he took treatment as a preventive of consumption which he thought he had inherited, and which he believed was manifesting itself. In Kissingen he met Julius Froebel, a nephew of the founder of the Kindergarten system, and himself deeply interested, not only in pedagogic matters, but in anything which concerned the social well-being of the masses. Froebel relates that Tolstoy gave expression to queer notions, among which was the thought that Russia would some day surpass Germany in educational matters ; "for the Russians," he said, "were yet an unspoiled people, while the Germans were like a child which for years had been receiving a wrong education." He communicated to Froebel his ideas of a new educational system, and the plans of a school, the beginning of which had already reached the experimental stage. The people were to him mystical beings, into whose depths no one had yet penetrated, and out of whom great and remarkable things were to come. He spoke sympathetically of communism; and in the labor trusts, which had their forerunners in Russian life, and are called "artels," he saw outlines of the future social world.

Disquieting news of his brother's condition came to him, and he went to Soden on the twentieth of August; arriving there, he found Nikolai so ill that his recovery was not expected. Tolstoy went with him to the south of France, where he died in his arms on the twentieth of September. Tolstoy's letter to his friend "Fyett" is written on the seventeenth of October, and is full of despair, evidently having been written under the influence of Schopenhauer, whom he was beginning to read and appreciate. He writes: "He literally died in my arms. Nothing in my life has made such an impression on me. He was right when he said, 'Nothing is worse than death;' and when one remembers that it is the end of everything, then there is also nothing worse than life. Why should one work and worry when of that which was Nikolai Tolstoy nothing remains? He did not say that he felt the coming of death, but I know that he was listening for its approaching steps and knew positively what was before him. A few minutes before he died he dozed ; suddenly he awoke with a start, and said, 'What was that?' He was beginning to feel his absorption into nothing; and if he found nothing on which to take hold,[1] what shall I find? Much less than he ; and assuredly I shall struggle with death as he has struggled. To the last minute he held on to life, did everything himself, tried to work, asked me about my plans, and gave me his advice. But I believe that he did all these things, not from a really natural impulse, but because of his principle. One thing remained with him to the end, — nature. The evening before he died he went into his room and sank exhausted upon his bed by the open window. I came to him, and he said to me, with tears in his eyes, 'What a happy hour I have had.' . . . 'Dust thou art, and to dust thou shalt return.' But one thing is left : the vague hope that in nature, of which we are a part on earth, something remains, and something will be found. All who saw Nikolai die, said, 'How peace-

---

[1] Nikolai's was a very religious nature.

fully he has passed away!' But I know what a torture death has been to him, because none of his feelings escaped me. A thousand times I say to myself, 'Let the dead bury their dead;' but what shall I do with the remaining strength? One cannot persuade a stone to change its course and fall upwards instead of to the earth whither it is drawn; one cannot laugh at a joke which has grown tedious; one cannot eat when the hunger is satisfied. To what purpose is everything, when to-morrow is to begin the death agony with all the mysteries of a lie, of self-deception, — and it all ends in nothing for you? Is n't it amusing? 'Be virtuous, be useful, happy, as long as you live,' say the people one to another, and you say that happiness and virtue have their root in truth. But the truth which I have discovered in my thirty-two years is, that life is terrible. You write, 'Take life as you find it, because you yourself are to blame for the position in which you find yourself.' I take life as I find it, but as soon as man has reached the highest plane of his development, the truth which he loves above everything else is awful. When one comes to see that clearly and plainly, he wakes, and says like my brother, 'What is that?' Yet it is plain that as long as one wishes to know the truth and to tell it, he endeavors to know it and to tell it; that is the only thing in the world of morals which remains for me, and higher I cannot go. This one thing I shall do; but not in your form of art. Art is a lie, and I cannot longer love a lie, although it is beautiful. . . . I shall remain here this winter; for, after all, it is the same thing where I live."

Thus deeply crushed, with views of life of a decidedly somber color, and a theory of his own art like that which he announces decades later in his "Confessions," he nevertheless gathered both courage and strength, left the Riviera and went to Geneva; from there again to Italy, through which he made an extended trip, and where he gave its art a more careful glance. In Marseilles, where he stopped on his way to Paris, he visited the public and industrial schools, and came in touch with the social movement of France.

From Paris he went to London. England always stood high in his estimation, although he did not like that type of the English which traverses the whole world and is disappointed if it does not find all of it to be a suburb of London. "It is the country of the noblest ideals and yet also of the coarsest materialism," Tolstoy said in a passing conversation; and from the idealistic standpoint it was to him the most sympathetic of any country in Europe. He felt himself especially attracted to Ruskin, and although they never met they were closely related in spirit. Both were aristocrats to their very finger-tips, and both were making the way straight for the coming of a democracy. Both were artistic natures, yet laid great stress upon the value of common labor. Both formulated theories of arts in which they were not masters, and which have caused much shaking of heads among the artists. Ruskin was as intense as Tolstoy, but not so concentrated; he was as religious but without being so rationalistic. In both of them the religious element is an important part, and both have interpreted it "in terms of human relations." Tolstoy attended a session in the House of Parliament. He visited the Tower and the dreadful East Side of London, where he saw civilization at its worst. He went to Brussels, where he remained but a short time, and, returning to

Russia by way of Germany, he visited Weimar, Gotha, and Eisenach. In Eisenach he climbed to the Wartburgh, — another Luther, he, born on a brighter day, in a darker country. In a visitor's book he wrote a sentence short and true : " Luther is great." Tolstoy and Luther are not so far apart as passing time has made them ; and they have fought upon the same battlefield with nearly the same weapons and the same enemy.

In 1861 Tolstoy was again in St. Petersburg ; and from there he went through Moscow to Yasnaya Polyana. With the full determination to make use of the experiences gathered abroad, he immediately asked the government for the privilege of establishing a public school in which he wished to develop his pedagogic ideas.

This year was an unfortunate one for Tolstoy, for it brought a complete severing of friendly relations with Turgenieff. The cause, as usual, was a trivial one. They were the guests of " Fyett " on his estate in Stepnakoff, and Turgenieff was telling of the education of his illegitimate daughter. He had engaged for her a governess who was very anxious to develop in her the altruistic feeling. " Now," he said, "she makes my daughter mend the clothes of the poor people." "And do you approve that?" asked Tolstoy. "Of course I do; it brings the child in touch with the real need of the people." "And I," replied Tolstoy hotly, "believe that a finely dressed child mending dirty clothes is simply performing a theatrical scene." "I won't let anybody talk that way to me," replied Turgenieff, not over-gently. "And why should I not say just what I think?" was Tolstoy's battle-cry. One word brought another, and the damage done was so great that a duel was talked of but fortunately averted. This little incident kept these two great men apart for nearly seventeen years, to their mutual regret; and both of them were to blame, although neither of them acknowledged it. The unprejudiced lookers-on cannot help putting more blame upon Tolstoy, whose exaggerated sense of truth knew no bounds, and who needlessly offended a great man and a loyal friend and admirer. Tolstoy suspected Turgenieff of professional jealousy; but there was never a trace of it in him, and he treated the younger man with the most generous respect. They were two opposite natures, as Turgenieff said : one of them, Turgenieff, a modern, a Westerner, and an artist, every fiber of his being in the present; and Tolstoy, although just as little a child of the past, eager to roll time backward, to turn away not only from all the achievements of civilization, but also from his own deeds and talents, to become "a voice in the wilderness."

He wrote this year the already spoken of "Cossacks," built upon material brought from the Caucasus; a shorter story, "Polikushka," which he regarded as "mere stuff" which "any man might write who could wield a pen." He also organized his school, published a pedagogic journal called "Yasnaya Polyana," made plans for new literary work, and held the office of justice of the peace, which was no sinecure, inasmuch as it meant settling the quarrels which arose after the liberation of the serfs, and the allotment of land to them. Tolstoy says: "Through that year I was justice of the peace, schoolteacher, journalist, and author, and nearly unnerved myself by the tasks, the struggle in my court was so great and my work in the school so unsatisfactory. My writing in the 'Journal,' talking one way and then another, which came from the desire to teach everybody and yet to hide the fact that I knew not what to teach, grew so repulsive to me that I threw the whole thing aside and went to the 'Steppes,' to the 'Bashkires,' to drink 'kumiss,' to breathe fresh air, and to lead a purely animal life." Strengthened, he returned from the "Steppes" in the south of Russia; the skies grew brighter, his courage had risen, his hold on life was stronger, and he began to think seriously of marriage; which was to end his dissatisfaction with life and bring the long-sought quiet and happiness.

CHAPTER IX

No human problem which pressed itself upon
Tolstoy was permitted to work itself out secretly.
"I have no secrets," he says ; "everybody may
know what I am doing ; " and from the first
perplexing questions which troubled the half-
awake brain of the child, through the whole
scale of human emotions, he permits us to listen
to him as he tries to answer or solve them.
With the same frankness with which he un-
covers the heart of the child and youth, he reveals the heart of the man who is beginning to
feel the joys and sorrows of his first true love.
When he tells in his story, "Family Happiness,"
of the growth of the love of Sergei Michaelovitsch for Mascha, the daughter of a childhood's
friend, he is simply telling the story of his own
love for Sofia Andreyevna, whose mother, a Russian woman, was his dear friend (and only about
a year and a half his senior), and whose father

was Dr. Baer, a German physician. Tolstoy was attracted to their home, not only by the friendship which bound him to the mother, but also because he found in its pure and hospitable atmosphere much of that which other houses lacked. Countess Tolstoy says that her husband was attracted to her parents' home because of its fine aristocratic spirit, while he maintains that it was because of the democratic principles which prevailed in it; for the daughters not only knew how to speak four languages fluently and play the piano artistically, but could supervise a household, and if necessary perform all the labor themselves.

Although Tolstoy was many years older than the young woman upon whom his choice had fallen, his love from the first was ardent and strong. He hesitated, however, to declare it, and his attentions were so general that the friends who kept a watchful eye upon him could not determine whether his visits were intended for the mother or the daughters, and, if for the daughters, for which one. The burdens by which he had loaded himself grew greater every day; the government had looked with suspicion upon his schools, the problem of developing his own life according to his high standards grew more difficult, and he yearned for the life of which he had long dreamed — "life by the side of a pure woman who would breathe peace upon him and who, while sharing his labor, would increase his joy." If ever a man thought of marriage "advisedly and soberly," it was Tolstoy; for although he was drawn to Moscow by that resistless power which he knew to be the power of love, he withstood the temptation to declare himself, and looked in silent admiration upon the young girl, in whom the promises of a beautiful womanhood were beginning to be fulfilled.

One day that same autumn a carriage drove into the park at Yasnaya Polyana, and out of it sprang three young women, who were followed by their mother, Mrs. Baer. They were on the way to their grandfather's estate, some fifty versts behind Yasnaya Polyana, and a short stop among their friends was as pleasant to them as it was to Tolstoy, to whom their presence brought great delight and seemed a fulfillment of his dreams. Sofia, the second daughter, was what we would call a tomboy, but without very much emphasis on the boy ; for she was womanly, graceful, and beautiful, yet as "playful as a kitten." She loved tennis and other outdoor sports, jumped over fences and ditches, climbed trees, and made the woods ring from her laughter. Somber old Yasnaya Polyana seemed to have been re-created by the presence of this young fairy, whose every step Tolstoy followed and upon whom his eyes rested fondly. For him there existed only two classes of women — "the one, which was composed of all the women in the world except Sofia, and who were heirs to all the feminine faults, just common human beings — and the other class, just her alone, without a fault and high above all others." Although no one knew that his attentions were centered upon her (and the mother thought that they were surely intended for her eldest daughter), Sofia, with that intuition which belongs to woman, had not only divined his love, but it had also awakened in her the same feeling.

Mrs. Baer and her daughters left Yasnaya Polyana after a three days' visit, and there was something in the glance of Tolstoy's eyes and in the pressure of his hand when he bade Sofia good-by which made his riding after them in a few days and his appearance at Ivizy quite natural and not unexpected to her. He came with the strong desire to ask Sofia to be his wife; and while they were alone under a shading tree, she sitting on a wooden bench in front of a table, he looking down on her chestnut-brown hair and into her grayish-blue eyes, the desire ripened into determination. She was playing with a piece of chalk, writing on the table, or rather just making marks, when he said : "I have been wishing to ask you something for a long time;" and the grayish-blue eyes looked into his, frightened but friendly, as she said: "Please ask." He took the piece of chalk out of her fingers, and wrote the first letters of the words of a sentence which was very complicated and which she had to decipher. "And what is this, and what is that?" he asked of one word after another; and with wrinkled forehead and blushing cheek she answered him. "And this word?" he asked again, and she said, "It means never, but it is not so;" and taking the crumbling chalk from him, she wrote four letters which did not form the

words of an intricate sentence, and he needed
no one to ask him, "What is this, or what is
that?" He knew what they meant; for all she
wrote was e-v-e-r. This declaration of his love he
used in a more complicated form in his "Anna
Karénina," where Levin thus declares himself
to Kitty, his future wife. While in the story the
mother seemed at first opposed to the union, in
reality it was the father, Dr. Baer, who bluntly
and definitely refused to give his consent. He
wished to see his oldest daughter married first;
and not until Tolstoy threatened to shoot himself if the father persisted in his refusal did he
yield.

Tolstoy wished to be married immediately; he
did not understand why he should have to wait
for the consummation of his wishes until the
trousseau was finished; and he begged off month
after month of the time set by Mrs. Baer, until
finally the 23d of September, 1862, was settled
upon as the date on which the ceremony was to
be performed. He went at everything connected
with the business of being married in an awk-
ward and reluctant fashion. His struggle was
especially great when he had to go to confes-

LEO TOLSTOY, JR.

The son who has literary tastes

sion, a matter which he had long neglected and in which he did not believe, but without which he could not marry. Yet he would have gone through the fire if it had been between him and his Sofia; so he went to the church and down upon his stiff knees, receiving absolution from the gentle, simple-minded priest, "who, indeed, could pull a tooth without hurting;" or, in other words, who could forgive sins without disturbing the conscience. Tolstoy listened to the service now absent-mindedly and now critically; for although he did not believe anything, he did not yet know but that he ought to; and while he denied his faith before the priest, he was not quite sure when he reached home whether, in trying to be perfectly honest, he had not after all told an untruth.

The day of the wedding found Tolstoy more nervous and excited than the cool-headed bride. He had to be ordered about like a school-boy, and was as much confused about the right and left hand as a raw Russian recruit who receives his first lesson in drilling. He felt deeply the quickly mumbled words of the priest; and the music of the invisible choir which repeated over and over

again, "Bless them, O Lord!" echoed in his
heart. "Eternal Lord," prayed the priest, "who
hast united that which was separated, who hast
made the indissoluble ties of love, and who
blessed Isaac and Rebecca, these are their descendants according to the covenant. Bless them,
these thy servants, Leo and Sofia, whom I myself bless ; for thou art a most merciful God, full
of love for men, and we praise thee, the Father,
and the Son, and the Holy Ghost, throughout
eternity, amen." The rings were exchanged, but
not without their first being mixed ; the priest
said, "We unite the servant of God, Leo, to the
handmaid of God, Sofia ; " and Tolstoy had entered into the long-looked-for harbor. "Fyett,
dear old boy, dearest friend," wrote Tolstoy,
intoxicated by his happiness, "I am married
two weeks and am a new, an entirely new crea-
ture."

Sofia entered completely into the thoughts and
plans of her husband. She was as idealistic as
he, but much more practical ; she took possession of keys and closets, brought order into confusion, and drove the leisurely horde of servants
and peasants into desperation, if not into a faster

gait. She had inherited from her father something of German thrift; and the rubles were not
permitted to roll out faster than the kopeks came
walking in. She kept the books and the cash, became general manager and overseer, and again
Tolstoy writes to "Fyett," "I have made an important discovery: Inspectors, overseers, and village
elders are a nuisance. I have done away with
them, and Sofia and I are way up to our eyes in
farming. We have bees, sheep, a new orchard,
and a distillery. I live in a world which lies so
far away from all literature and all criticism that
when I receive a letter like yours, my first
thought is one of astonishment and surprise
as to who has written 'The Cossacks,' or 'Polikushka'!"

In the summer of the next year "Fyett" came
on a visit to which he had been repeatedly urged;
and he paints in glowing colors the idyllic picture which he saw. Dressed in a light gown,
Sofia came running to meet him among the white
birches, a sapling herself; Tolstoy was at the
pond, catching crabs which they had for supper.
Everything was bright, hopeful, full of life and
full of peace. It was a glorious evening which

he spent with them ; there was no trace of any pressing problem, and no weighty questions were discussed. It was just life at its best; a self-effacing life in which Tolstoy forgot himself and all the problems of existence.

The young couple was not spared some dis-illusions, for Tolstoy was still very human and his wife had never pretended to be anything else. He loved her passionately and trusted her im-plicitly ; yet he was jealous, and when the yellow monster controlled him most, he looked every-where for an imaginary lover, and then was heartily ashamed of himself. On the 28th of June, 1863, their eldest child was born. With its first cry Tolstoy awoke from his dream, and the old questioning spirit began to torment him again about the meaning of life and its develop-ment. Neither his happy marriage nor the birth of his child could fill so large a life completely ; nor did the teaching in the schools and writing his pedagogic journal satisfy him.

"The Linen-Measurer" is the only thing he wrote during the early part of his married life. It is the story of a horse which philosophizes about property, society, and humanity in general ;

and grew out of Tolstoy's love for horses and his critical attitude toward society. So artistically is this done that one scarcely realizes the fact that it is impossible for a poor, halting horse to think so logically and intelligently. Tolstoy has the same love for animals that characterizes the Russian mujik, who makes household pets of them, and lives so close to his stock that he and they grow like one another, — patient, slow, and meditative. Walking through the markets of Moscow with a friend, Tolstoy pointed to the small, unkempt, good-natured horse which stood among the pots and kettles that the mujik had brought to the market, and noticed this very resemblance. He never passed a horse without petting it, and when it was ill-treated he felt for it as for a human being.

The years up to 1877 were filled by diligent work : the writing of his longest two stories, the looking after his estate, which he tried to improve in every way possible, teaching in the public schools, and, what was the most important, training his own children. "War and Peace," which took five years for completion, needed constant and painstaking historical study ;

but books were far away and difficult to get. The Russian censor kept strict watch upon everything that breathed thought from the printed page. The libraries in Moscow which were well stocked by historic books were always in confusion; for there was no catalogue (neither is there yet one, although it has been coming for some thirty years), and Tolstoy had to work painfully and laboriously. His most productive time was winter, or when winter was passing away, when the huts of the peasants began to be thawed out from the surrounding snow. Spring brought the cares of the farm, which were constantly growing greater; for in the measure in which he tried to carry on the work intelligently, the peasants grew more stupid and less reliable. When he wrote to " Fyett " about the progress of his stories, he never forgot to mention his timothy and clover, or his sick horse, and to ask for this or that favor, from the buying of a rope to an agricultural implement. When spring came, which in Russia does not come like a " dancing psaltress," but like a troop of rough, boisterous boys, his thoughts turned ardently toward that side of nature which cannot be plowed or sown; and in imagination he saw the coming summer in all its beauty. "A friend is good, but Nature is better; she is a friend whom one does not lose in death, for when one dies he is completely re-united with her." He feels that Nature is the one thing that connects him with the higher world; and "if one were not conscious of her, so that in stumbling one can catch hold of her, life were an evil thing indeed."

Tolstoy grew mentally lazy in the summer; the physical and mental joys were so great that he forgot or neglected the pen. Visitors came flocking during that season, and although he jealously guarded his time and strength, he was always a genial host, who thought it his duty to entertain the company, and always was the soul of it. "Fyett" writes to him that he is alone, and he replies, somewhat fretfully, "Fortunate man to be alone. I have a wife, three children, and a baby, all of whom are sick. Fever and heat, headaches, coughs," the whole catalogue of infants' diseases, had descended upon them and kept him from work. He is glad when visitors come, even if only to quarrel with them; and he does quarrel with most of them, although good-naturedly. Often he complains: "I am doing nothing; it is a dull, dead time with me; I do not think or write, but feel myself pleasantly stupid." This stupidity was in reality his period of ripening; thoughts crowded his brain thick and fast, and he absorbed them like a sponge. He read much of the German, French, and English classics, but they made no impression upon him. Schopenhauer came to him like a revelation, and he was astonished that no one had discovered that pessimistic genius; unless it was, as Schopenhauer so often says, that "besides idiots, there are no human beings in the world."

The next year Tolstoy began the study of classic languages, a matter which he had neglected in his youth, and in which he now found much pleasure. "From morning till night," he writes, "I learn Greek and do nothing else. I now read Xenophon at sight, although for Homer I use a dictionary, as it gives me a little trouble. I am happy that God has sent me this foolish notion. First of all, I find real pleasure in it; secondly, I realize that I never knew what beautiful and what beautifully simple things have

been created by the words of man ; and, thirdly,
I do not and shall not write mere verbiage."
The intense study of the Greek, which was followed by the study of Hebrew, brought on an
illness, and for a time it looked as if the dreaded
consumption had fastened itself upon him. He
went to Samara to drink kumiss, and returned
strengthened, ready for the greater work before
him. Following his illness came the death of the
youngest boy ; treacherous croup had choked
out the little life, bringing sorrow and sadness to
Tolstoy, but especially to his wife, who, in spite
of her physical strength, suffered deeply from
this affliction, upon which still others were to
follow.

Tolstoy's aunt, Tatyana Alexandrovna, died
not quite a year afterwards, and he writes : "She
died slowly and gradually. I have been used to
death ; nevertheless, hers was, as is the death
of each person who is near and dear to us, a new
and terrible experience." It was to him like
losing his mother ; for she had been with him
from his earliest years until he left her to go to
the university. Another child, a ten-months-old
baby, died during the same year, so that the

angel of death had scarcely turned from their door until he came again.

The education of the children was no little task, and one which was entered into with much thought, but in which the parents were not a unit. The Countess did not wish her children to serve as an experiment, and they received the customary education in the usual manner, through tutors and governesses. It is true that much liberty was given them, that they were not driven to their tasks, and that they were the constant companions of their parents ; but the method was a compromise, and brought none but the customary results. Strong as Tolstoy was in his convictions, he did not feel that he should force his wife and children into his way of thinking; and at Yasnaya Polyana it was soon the fashion for every one to go his own way. Friends of the family call this coming and going and do-as-you-please fashion the " Tolstoy style "; and it has its advantages as well as its disadvantages.

Countess Tolstoy was in many respects a model wife, and to be the wife of a genius is no easy task. Uncomplainingly and joyfully, she bore

MARIA LEVOVNA

The second daughter

him thirteen children in twenty-seven years, nursing all of them but one herself. She was their companion and friend, and nine of them grew into manhood and womanhood by her side. For love of her husband she buried herself with him in Yasnaya Polyana, until she thought that for the sake of the children they must move to Moscow. She went with him through every phase of his moral and spiritual development, and stopped short only when to continue would have endangered the educational and social standing of the children. One cannot blame her for stopping just where she did stop, but one cannot help regretting it. True it is that the children might have grown up like peasants; but they would have been the sires of such a peasantry as Russia has never known, and of which it is sorely in need. Nine such peasants would have stood like strong pillars in a new social temple, while they are now nine aristocrats among ninety thousand or more of their kind, no worse and no better than the others. Among the sons, Leo, Jr., alone has literary tendencies and some talent. He has written a number of plays, and in one of them his father discovers real dramatic power, although

the public does not seem to share this opinion.
He is married to an excellent Danish woman and
lives in St. Petersburg, where he is endeavoring
to be of some public service. Another son is an
official of the government, while the others
have married rich wives. Two of the daughters
have married nobles of the highest rank; so
that nearly all his children have gone over into
the camp of his sworn enemies. During these
years Tolstoy was beginning to know that he was
made of the stuff of which martyrs are made;
and martyrs and reformers ought never to marry.
No man can press a thorny crown upon the head
of the wife and the children he loves; and a wife
of Countess Tolstoy's tender and devoted nature
can always slip a piece of velvet under her husband's crown just where he wishes it to press
most heavily. She always knew what he needed,
even if he did not wish it, and although he was
beginning to sway the world by his thought, he
was often swayed by her thoughtfulness. Had
Tolstoy married a woman less practical, less devoted to the material side of his interest, and less
careful of everything that concerned his health
and comfort, he would no doubt have died long

ago ; but many people ask themselves whether he would not have lived longer ; for he would have died either a victim of his enemies or a sacrifice to his principles ; and these insure a longer immortality than being cuddled in a soft bed and living beyond the allotted threescore years and ten.

CHAPTER X

THE difference between a Russian aristocrat and a peasant is social, rather than cultural as it is in Poland, for instance, where the two seem to belong to separate races and nowhere have a point of contact. In Russia they are more closely related than the aristocrat allows, or the peasant knows. They are "chips of the same block"; the one carved and polished, and not always thoroughly, the other rough and crude, lying just where he fell; and the two are an immeasurable distance apart. In Tolstoy they seemed to meet; for he is the finest product of the Russian aristocracy, and feels himself drawn toward it, although he resists the attraction as best he can resist it. At the same time his love for the soil, for the homely peasant and his homelier beasts, manifests itself strongly in him, and he was the first to cry out: "Take your feet from the body of the peasant; for you are trampling on your own flesh." He was quick to see the unspoiled good in him, and for the good which was spoiled he felt himself and his class responsible.

The Russian peasant is, like all Russians and all other human beings, more or less, a big bundle of contrasts. He is faithful and suspicious, honest and false, simple-minded yet shrewd, industrious and lazy, good-natured yet a furious fighter. He is one of Russia's many unsolved problems and unfinished products which Tolstoy felt it his duty to help solve and finish. On the 19th of February, 1861, during his absence abroad, the edict which liberated the serfs had been signed and the difficult task of readjustment was about to begin. As most of the serf-owners looked upon the emancipation of the serfs as ruinous to themselves and the peasantry, the government found in them a great unwillingness to obey the new and revolutionary law. A few, including Tolstoy, had set their serfs free before the law was passed; but to the majority it was a greater hardship than was the freeing of the slaves for the Southerners, as the Russians not only had to give up their human property but also much land, for which, however, they were

to be recompensed; but the payment was to
be slow and long drawn out. Each peasant
was to begin his new existence as a land-owner,
and to the former serf-owners themselves was
intrusted the task of reorganization. Tolstoy
was appointed by the Senate as one "mirovoy,"
or justice of the peace, before whom differences
were adjusted and quarrels laid aside. To him it
was no empty honor, nor was he unfitted for the
office; for he was strong yet tender, he had an
abnormal sense of right and yet was peace-loving.
He was a splendid organizer, and it is fair to say
that the peasants in his district, although they
were judged by a superior, were served as by
one of their own number. There was no little
complaint made by the owners of the "souls," as
the serfs were called, because of his partiality
towards them; and although he tried to be perfectly just to both parties, he had small patience
with those of his neighbors who saw in the
mujik an inferior being, born for servitude only.
The peasants were also hard to manage, for they
had no idea of the difference between mine and
thine, and when it came to the division of property, they could not see why they might not

have this piece of land as well as that, or why this noble could not dispense with a particular bit of meadow which they desired. Once very servile, they now tried to take the bit into their own mouths and run away, quite unconscious of the fact that they were still passengers in the cart which they were pulling and that the only fundamental difference between their new relation and the old one was that now they would be paid for the pulling, while formerly they got but scant food and much whipping if the master was so inclined.

Tolstoy saw in the serfs' emancipation a fulfillment of his own desires, but could not help feeling disappointed later as to its material results for the peasants. He never thought that this humane act came too soon, but he felt after a few years that the peasants were not quite capable of taking care of themselves. They had a chance to buy land but did not do so; they could easily have increased their stock, but instead of that it decreased; the soil which they might have improved grew more impoverished; and when they should have aided one another in their new communal life, selfishness as well as poverty increased. The freeing of the serfs did not quite solve the problem, because the product, the peasantry, had to be finished first, and Tolstoy continued with still greater ardor the education of that incomplete, overgrown child, the mujik. Tolstoy had begun his educational experiment very young, when he knew but little about pedagogic principles and was not aware that the organization of private schools was not permitted by the government. He had gone abroad largely to study the schools in the west of Europe, quite unconsciously obeying the almost universal principle that "nations go West to study, and East to teach." In 1859 he organized two schools near his estate, and when he returned in 1861 a third one was added. He had brought with him a German assistant and four university students from Moscow, whom he had trained for this special task. In December of the same year a fourth school had to be opened ; and before long Tolstoy was the superintendent, principal, and teacher of twelve schools, which he constantly visited and in which he taught the Russian language, singing, drawing, and Biblical history. The central school was at Yasnaya Polyana, in a wing of his residence, and consisted of two rooms, a physical cabinet, and adjoining them two living-rooms for the teachers. Manual training was also attempted, and a carpenter's bench stood in the hall above, while in the one below it was a crude gymnastic apparatus.

The first principle which Tolstoy announced was that there should be absolutely no compulsion used anywhere in any way. Perfect liberty was the watchword ; if the peasant did not care to go to school, it simply proved that the educational system, as well as its product, was unsatisfactory. "What right have we," he says in his pedagogic journal, " to force a peasant to study, when we do not quite know what or how to teach ? The West has a method which has an historic development, and it can be defended upon that ground; but in Russia we do not know yet what is good and what is ill." There was to be no imitating any method ; there was, indeed, to be no method, or, as he puts the whole matter tersely, " The only method of education is to experiment ; the only standard, Liberty." Or somewhat more clearly he says again, " The public schools should meet the needs of the people ; but what these needs are can only be discovered by studying them and experimenting upon them." His school was conducted in this way : at eight o'clock in the morning a bell was rung by one of the boys who slept in the school ; for in winter not all the children could return to their homes. The bell was a signal and not a call, and who would come, came. If they were in time, well and good ; if they were tardy, no one noticed it. They carried nothing in the shape of books, as all the work was done in the schoolroom and not much of it out of books. The children could make all the noise they wished to, and they took full advantage of the privilege, although not any more than in some schools where they are supposed to be "seen and not heard." Nor did the noise subside when the teacher appeared ; and when he opened the desk to distribute the books and writing materials they rushed at him, each one eager to get his own first. The seats were not assigned according to any method, but each child sat just where he chose ; some sat on the floor, others stood near the teacher's desk, and all did just as they pleased. Children of one neighborhood naturally flocked with one another, and the girls also naturally drifted toward each other. They stayed in the school-room seven hours; but of these so many were filled by apparent play and so few by work that no one found them too long. Russian history and religion were taught in one room, and all the children attended those classes together. Although there was a regular schedule, it was seldom adhered to; for the teacher allowed himself the same liberty which he gave to the children. He taught as long as he thought that they cared for a subject, and often prolonged a lesson because they were in the "swing" of it; while another theme was no sooner begun than it was changed because the school was not in the mood for it. When the children were most interested, as in reading or history, they crowded close to the teacher in pellmell fashion; although by instinctive courtesy the girls and the smaller boys were permitted to stand closest to him.

When Tolstoy entered a room everything stopped, and the pupils surrounded him begging for a story; for the children knew him to be a splendid story-teller, and they listened to him as attentively as did the grown-ups the world over. Many of his best folk-tales have their origin in these school-room visits, and he frankly acknowledges that the children helped him to make them. He told them about his imprisonment in the Caucasus, his adventures with bears, described the antics of his favorite dogs, retold according to Russian taste the "Arabian Nights," and wrote for them what is regarded as one of his finest folk-tales, "God sees the truth, though He does not tell it at once." A primer which he wrote at that time has gone through twenty editions, and is still popular with the people as well as with the educators. If the weather was good, Tolstoy and the children ran out of the school-room into the woods, to the meadow, or the pond. They bathed and fished together, and in the winter made snow-men or pelted one another with snowballs. The foremost boy among them was Tolstoy himself, who was the leader in all their pranks.

This method, although he did not permit it to be called that, attracted and received its full share of criticism. A school without law, order, or schedule, and with teachers and principals who behaved themselves like little boys, was something to be severely condemned. The one criticism which both the state and the individual made in common was, that pupils from such a school could not be trained to be good subjects of an autocratic government, or desirable children of parents who exacted obedience. Tolstoy replied that it was not the business of his schools to train, but to educate ; that training rested upon force and law, and had its reason in the state, the church, the family, and society as they were organized. " It is reasonable," he said, "that the state wishes to train, for it needs men for various purposes to fit into the niches already built for them ; the church also wants the children trained, so that they may obey and believe ; so does the family, because it wishes the children to grow into something of the same fashion as the parents." Society, he claimed, desired children trained in a certain way, for no healthful purpose, but simply to satisfy the pride of the human mind. Consequently its methods bear the most dangerous fruit : such as universities and university training. He judged all such institutions by those of Kazan and Moscow, and their fruits by the educated

proletariat which they created, and so came to
the conclusion that universities serve no good
purpose. "For they do not spring from any
real need felt by the people, they do not train
those necessary to humanity, but only such as a
corrupted society needs." The West, he declared,
had universities because they grew and developed with the people, and perhaps served their
purpose; but the East had its development still
before it, and one does not know just what universities it will need, if any. To Tolstoy, Russia
was a world apart, which could healthfully develop only according to the character of its people, whom he considered radically different from
those in the West; a thought that has served
to strengthen the Slavophilic movement which
makes this its chief doctrine, but in a much
less humble spirit.

While Tolstoy did not believe in training a
child, he believed in its education, which he
thinks should be based upon the individuality
of the child, and therefore should give the completest liberty. "The school is not to have rigid
schedules and far-reaching plans; but every
science is to be studied and taught in the

completest freedom, and it will gradually and harmoniously adjust itself to the needs of men. The school, then, is not an institution in which to train children, or to force knowledge upon them, but it is to influence the child definitely ; and influence is without force."

He pictures a school in which everything which a child instinctively dreads shall be absent. No high desk for the teacher, no straight, monotonous rows of benches, no long wastes of blackboards before which children feel themselves so small and insignificant. His ideal is that everything should constantly change with the needs and tastes of the children. A school as he saw it was to be a kindergarten, university, museum, theater, picture-gallery, forest, library, and meadow, all blending into one. This was indefinite enough ; but it had in it the pedagogic ideals of the future. Tolstoy knew that his plans were idealistic and that the coming generations would cling to their institutions as they found them, " upon the principle of the sick man who said : ' The medicine has been bought, therefore I must drink it.' "

More radical than his method of education,

and in greater contrast to present standards, was his view of its aim and purpose. Markff, the inspector of the Latin School in Tula, a very excellent pedagogue and a personal friend of Tolstoy's, wrote a criticism of his school in which he says, in brief, that "Upon the education of the younger generation by the old, upon the communication of its views and conclusions to the younger generation, which give it a basis for development, upon these rests the progress of humanity." In answer to which Tolstoy comes out bluntly, and says: "I do not believe in this progress, it is not a universal law; progress is not always necessary, nor is it always good. Progress in one direction is paid for by a backward step in another. In Russia only the useless classes believe in progress; nine tenths do not believe in it; for it does not add anything to their happiness. The peasant does not need the telegraph, or the railroads which entice him from the country to the city, neither does he need the printing-press; he is not quite sure that reading does not spoil him. We must believe the peasants more than we do society; for they are in the majority and without them society cannot

live ; but the peasant can live without society."
He does not believe in progress, and therefore
does not think that one generation has a right
to interfere in the education of the next. Here
it was pointed out that Tolstoy overrated the
peasant, and, moreover, that he acted contrary
to his principle, the very existence of his school
being the proof of it. He defines education as
" A human activity which has back of it a desire
for equality in knowledge, and the fundamental
law of the self-progression of knowledge." Finally, he came to this conclusion : " We must go
to school to the children and not the children to
us." Their simplicity and honesty, their native
intuitions, their great thoughts, which sprang up
quite unconsciously, his great love for them, by
which he measured all their virtues, his love for
everything natural, and his abhorrence for everything artificial, made him echo the saying of a
prophet of long ago : " A little child shall lead
them." He studied them intently ; the birth of
each thought, its formation into speech, its trans-
ference to paper ; all this he felt through and
through ; becoming as much as possible " like
the least of these little ones," he saw their

kingdom. He found in them the creative power of the artist, and full of astonishment he cries out : "I was surprised and frightened when I made this discovery; I felt like a treasure-seeker who has discovered the magic root by which he will find the prize he desired; or as one who comes suddenly upon the Stone of Wisdom which he has sought incessantly for years." One story which has appeared among his works is the product of these children, and is called "Soldier's Life." It is the biography of a boy whose drunken father is sent away among the soldiers and who comes home a new man. Tolstoy thinks that nothing better than this has been written in Russian literature, and he bases his opinion upon the fact of its naturalness and simplicity. He felt the Old Testament to be a great source of inspiration, and the children disclosed to him its simple grandeur. He says: "I tried to teach them the New Testament, geography, the history of Russia, and natural history; everything was easily forgotten, and listened to rather unwillingly. Only the Old Testament remained in their memories, was listened to delightedly, and retold by them when they reached their homes. It stayed with them to this degree, that, after two months, they could, with only a few mistakes, write down what they had heard. I believe that the Old Testament, this book of the childhood of the race, will always remain the best book for the childhood of every man." Tolstoy does not believe in expurgated or abridged editions of the Scripture, but thinks it should be read by every child, with all its secret and sacred thoughts and its great and lofty poetry, which bring him under the enchantment of this new and old world, and which awaken in him the desire to develop himself. To Tolstoy it is the power which lifts the curtain before the child, who willingly enters that world and reaches out after the New Testament, after the history of his own country, and the sciences of nature. " There is no book like the Bible to open to the child this new world, and to hold him to love and to knowledge. I mean this also for those who do not believe it to be a revelation. I do not know a book which gives in such compact and poetic form every phase of human ideas as the Bible. All the questions which arise out of the manifestations of nature have their answer here ; all the original relations of man to man, the family, the state, religion, are known for the first time through this book. The power of truth, and wisdom in its simple, childish form, take hold of the child's mind with their powerful charm. The Psalms of David influence not only the thought of the child, but he learns to know for the first time the whole fascination of poetry in its inimitable purity and strength. Who of us has not wept over the story of Joseph and his brethren, or listened to the story of the shorn Samson with much anxiety and beating of the heart ; and who has not received all those other hundreds of noble impressions which we have drawn in as with our mother's milk ? I repeat it," he says, " without the Bible the education of the child in the present state of society is impossible."

Strange, new, revolutionary, and impracticable as was Tolstoy's pedagogic activity, it worked untold good, and it was due not to his method or lack of it, but to his deep, pure, and unselfish love for every child that touched him. The school was a family, and it was remarkably fortunate in its father. Each child was to him a perfect work of the Creator; he did not believe that it was "vile and full of sin." He believed implicitly, with One greater than himself, who put a little child in the midst, and said of it, "Except ye become as this little child, ye shall in no wise enter into the Kingdom of Heaven." That kingdom he considered the goal of the race; and all education had to prepare for it, even if the child was not lifted one inch toward what men call progress. These simple thoughts were still wrapped in much philosophic verbiage; but little by little they unwound themselves from their binding grave-clothes, to stand out clear and vivid, the goal of his own life as well as that of the human family, in which he was beginning to feel himself "the chief of sinners," and "not the least among the apostles."

CHAPTER XI

IT was no wonder that Tolstoy's health suffered during the period of his manifold activities. He was judge, teacher, farmer, journalist, and "last but not least," author. Quietly, like a miner in the depths, and just as painfully, he worked, gathering his material for a large historic novel which was to be called "The Decembrists," and based upon the suppressed political rising in December, 1825, the year in which Nicholas I. ascended the throne. Tolstoy's personal acquaintance with some of the participants in the movement led him to the consideration of that theme. One chapter was written and the whole fairly well sketched when, in studying the period which led to this little upheaval, he came upon that great, dark, and terrible picture of the Napoleonic invasion. It so fascinated him, as it fascinates every one who reads the history of Russia or of France, that he cast aside the subject and the material

172

of the first story and began his "War and Peace," to which he gave five years of preparation, but which was written and finished in a surprisingly short time. In November, 1864, he writes to "Fyett" : "I am much downcast and do not write at all; nevertheless, I am working really painfully. You cannot imagine how hard this preparation is; this deep plowing of the soil upon which I am driven to cast my seed. To consider and reconsider what will happen to these human beings of my story, which is to be a huge work, to think out millions of possibilities and then choose the millionth part of them, is tremendously difficult."

In 1865 he could already announce to "Fyett" the completion of the first part; and he writes thus : "These days there is being printed the first half of the first volume of my story. Please let me know what you think of it. You will see that everything that I have written thus far was only trivial; but that which I have now written I think more of. I am glad that you like my wife, but alas! I now love her less than I do my novels;" and he adds, also jokingly, "The greater I grow, the less I love you."

In November, 1866, he writes again to this same friend, who was always a very conscientious critic, " In your last letter you tell me some very interesting things concerning my novel. I am quite satisfied by what you say of my hero Prince Andrey ; he is a tedious, monotonous fellow, and only in the first part is he *comme il faut.* You are right about that, but it is my fault and not his. Besides the characters and their movements and meetings one with the other, I still have to work on the historic part, and I doubt that I shall be able to pull through. I have recognized my fault and hope that I have corrected it to your satisfaction. Please, dear friend, let me know just what you find wrong in my story."

In 1869 the work was finished ; and upon its publication it was hailed by Russian critics as the greatest novel of the nineteenth century. This was superlative praise, but praise in which readers and critics the world over almost unanimously agreed. His great talent is seen not only in the portraiture of classes and individuals, which is done with a rare fidelity, but by the ease with which the whole is written, and which nowhere betrays the fact that back of it is much hard study, and all through it the most painstaking labor. Turgenieff, who was not a biased critic, wrote of it : "'War and Peace' is the most poetic and artistic, the most beautiful and complete work which has appeared in our literature." When another Russian critic writes that "the story has no rival in the whole world," we detect just a little exaggeration ; but he is perfectly right when he says : "This work is a splendid picture of the struggle of our whole nation. Marvelous is Tolstoy's knowledge of the character of the Russian people, the clearness and purity of his views of life, and the historic and philosophic importance of his characters. He has reproduced the whole epoch to the satisfaction of the historians, who believe it to be scientifically correct."

While the work has no scientific connection with his former stories, which were largely biographical, or at least of his own time, it is closely related to them. It represents Tolstoy's mental and spiritual progress as he speaks now through one and now through another of his characters, many of whom were patterned after his relatives who had a part in that famous struggle. The critics, including Turgenieff, found fault with his mysticism and with his emphasis upon religious and philosophical problems which are woven through this book, and which seem a little didactic and out of place. No one, however, can write a story of the Russian people without discussing these questions; especially during a crisis, when such thoughts filled the Russian mind. Napoleon was to the people the "Antichrist," the war a punishment, and the victory the return of God's favor. Nearly everything which Napoleon did not destroy, be it a holy picture, a shrine, or a monastery, has remained to them a proof of the divine miracle. To-day one may have pointed out to him, by fairly intelligent people, a picture of the Virgin, in the Kreml, at which it is said a soldier shot, and the bullet was deflected in a miraculous way, killing the iconoclast himself.

"War and Peace" is the history of three aristocratic families widely different from one another, but altogether making a composite picture of Russian society. We see them in their palaces in St. Petersburg, in the fashionable salons of Moscow, in the seclusion of their country homes. We meet them at the chase, in their

social intrigues, in field and forest, in the draw-
ing-room, and in the splendor of their feasts and
festivals. Roused from their lethargy and weaned
from their luxuries, we see them again on the
battlefield in the thick of the fight, in camp by the
flickering watch-fires, with their backs toward the
victorious foe. In Moscow we see them once more
starving and pale in the lurid light of that con-
flagration which destroyed a city but saved a
nation ; and at last in the deep, cold snow, the
pall of the French army in its flight to France.

Count Ilya Rostoff is that type of the Russian
aristocrat, unfortunately not rare, who is born
"bon-vivant and epicure." Everything which he
does not care to study he dismisses and solves
by saying: "Splendid." Of culture he knows nothing, of gastronomy everything. The intricate
mixture of a sauce, the roasting of a prairie
chicken, are his fields of investigation, and
with them his brain and teeth are busy. He has
debts from which he will never be able to free
himself, nor does he greatly care to do so. He
reaches bottom very soon, but never ceases to
be a good father, and (what is somewhat more
remarkable in that sphere of Russian society),

a faithful husband, although his wife is ill and exceedingly nervous. They have four children : Vera, Nikolai, Natasha, and little Petya. Nikolai is a soldier, somewhat stupid and slow, who seldom departs from a safe and well-beaten track. Natasha grows from playing with dolls to the longing for real love, a romantic but pure-minded and extremely affectionate child. " She was so happy after her first ball that she thought every human being good, and did not believe in the possibility of evil, misfortune, and sorrow."

The Karagins, the second family, represent in the head of its household the materialistic aristocrat who measures everything by the standard of its money value and its possibility of serving him for his own aggrandizement. Cold, calculating, and without feeling, he plays his part in life and plays it well. Of his two sons, one is stupid, and the other mad from excesses, thinking only of new spoil for his pleasures. To him life is a series of entertainments which some one is in duty bound to provide for him. He is the logical son of such a father, and to be found to-day in countless editions in the pleasure haunts of which Moscow and St. Petersburg have a

TATYANA SEVORNA

The oldest daughter

good share, and a poor type, and in which these sons scatter the fortunes of their fathers. The daughter Hélène fits well into this atmosphere of the flesh, being a future adulteress, whom Napoleon splendidly characterized by saying : *" C'est un superb animal."* Pierre Besuchoff, the illegitimate son of an exceedingly wealthy father, comes under the influence of Hélène and her tricky relatives, and marries her after having inherited his father's millions and some forty thousand serfs. Pierre is near-sighted in more than one way, absent-minded and angular, seeming out of place in that society into which the Karagins have drawn him. He bluntly tells just what he thinks, nearly driving his diplomatic hostesses into desperation by his frankness.

Far away from the tumult of the city and the fashionable crush of its salons, we meet Prince Bolkonsky, the head of the third family. He belongs to that real aristocracy, rare in every country, rarer in Russia ; an aristocracy which, it is true, is very proud, but which has good reason to be so. The Prince has been banished to his estate on account of his political ideas, and although the term of his exile has long passed, he remains

just where he was sent ; for, he says, "If they
want me at court, let them send for me." They
do need him, and the chief dignitaries of
Russia come and ask his assistance in the war
then in progress. He is a man who is severe
toward his subordinates, among whom one must
count his daughter Marya, whom he loves in
his haughty way, and who always prays, before a meeting between herself and her father,
that it may pass off peacefully. If she has
a thought of rebellion she blames herself, and
thinks that she has sinned. She is very homely,
like nearly all the good people portrayed by Tolstoy, who, if he were to paint or describe the
Christ, would no doubt do so after the manner
of the prophet Isaiah, as "A root out of a dry
ground : he hath no form nor comeliness ; and
when we shall see him, there is no beauty that
we should desire him." But Marya with all her
homeliness is beautiful, because out of her large
blue eyes shines the love of Christ, " who suffered
because he loved men, although he was God."
Marya's aim and desire are to bless all who hate
her and despitefully use her, and to serve all
who need her. "For all the intricate laws of

human society she finds a solution in the law of
love and self-sacrifice." Her brother Andrey is
as proud as his father, but more ambitious. War
is a field from which to mount to glory ; so he
leaves his wife, with whom he is not very happy,
and joins the staff of General Kutusoff. Splendid,
and characteristic of father and son, is their
parting. "Now, farewell." He turned his cheek
to the son for a kiss, and embracing him said :
" Remember this one thing, Prince Andrey : if
you fall I shall suffer." He was silent a moment,
then suddenly cried out : " But if I hear that you
have not carried yourself like the son of Nikolai
Bolkonsky, I shall be ashamed." "That you
need not tell me, father," said the son, smiling.

Wounded upon the battlefield, looking into the
deep sky, he feels the presence of the unknown
God, and becomes conscious of his own soul. He
says, after reasoning much about it, "There is
nothing so sure as the nothingness of everything
which I have understood, and the greatness of
that which I do not understand, but which is
more important." Believed by his relatives to be
dead, he returns at the critical moment when
his wife gives birth to a son, and her own life

passes into the great beyond. After that he buries himself on his estate, wishing to forget and be forgotten. Pierre, the husband of Hélène, is unhappy in another way; his wife is not loyal to him, and he fights a duel with her paramour. At the time when life seems such a great puzzle, and everything soulless and material as a stone, he meets a Freemason who attracts him by his ethical views, which are to him a revelation and which he accepts. He becomes an ardent member of the lodge, returns home, and visits Prince Andrey, whom he is able to awaken from his lethargy to a realization of his duty to his fellow men. Natasha Rostoff, whom Andrey loves, is nearly ruined by Anatol, Hélène's brother, and Pierre rescues her from the impending danger. Andrey returns to the field at Borodino, and the evening before the battle, apprehensive as to its outcome, he looks back upon his life and sees clearly the vanity of all his ambitions. Coarse and crude seem those flights of his imagination which had always been so alluring to him — "Fame, patriotism, altruism, woman's love;" and now everything pales before the white light of that morning which is rising for him.

His apprehensions are justified, and he is severely wounded. While he is being cared for, he hears next to him weeping and lamentation, and recognizes Anatol, the would-be betrayer of Natasha; but instead of hate, he feels love for him, in spite of the fact that he is his greatest enemy. Instead of the feeling of revenge, there rises in him the feeling of pity, and he has an affection for all men, whom he now knows to be his brothers, whether they love or hate him. He feels the love and pity which his sister Marya had taught him, and which he never understood. Yes, he will live that love, but now it is too late; yet not too late, for that divine love never ceases, never can be destroyed. "Love is the essence of the soul." He is taken back to Moscow, from which every one is fleeing. The Rostoffs are just leaving the city; and Natasha persuades her parents to take into their wagon some of the wounded soldiers, although to do so they must leave their valuables behind. Thus it happens that, by the light of the destructive fire which consumed Moscow, Natasha and her lover meet, not to part again until he succumbs to his wounds. Marya, his sister, and Natasha, through being together at his bedside, learn to love each other with that pure love which always emanated from Andrey's sister.

Pierre is an idle looker-on at the battle of Borodino, but it has great consequences for him also. He is fired by the bravery of the Russian soldiers, is roused from his indifference, and thinks that he will free his country by one stroke, — the assassination of Napoleon. Before he can come near the execution of his plans he is arrested, and is in danger of being executed as one of the incendiaries. In prison he meets a common Russian soldier, Platon Karatayeff, who through his conduct communicates to him a philosophy of life. "He lived in love," Tolstoy says of him. "Not in love to one certain person, but to all human beings whom he met. He loved his comrades, he loved the French, he loved Pierre, he loved even his little dog." Platon is shot by the French because he is incapable of marching ; but he continues to live in Pierre, who is a changed man. Natasha says of him to her friends, "He is so clean, so new, so fresh, as if he were coming out of a bath ; you understand, out of a moral bath."

TOLSTOY THE MAN

In this story, whose history unrolls itself in such an interesting and tragic way, and which ends happily in Pierre's marriage to Natasha, and Nikolai Rostoff's to the Princess Marya, the characters are but the mouthpieces for Tolstoy's view of life, which was coming near the point of ripening into a definite philosophy, and of being formulated into a sociology. He says: "In notable, historic movements, the so-called great men are the labels, which name events and periods; but, just like the labels, they have the least to do with the events." To Tolstoy, the hero of former days, the man who reaped all the glory, and did nothing, had no right to exist. To him the masses were the real hero; to him there is no science of warfare; and victory and defeat, everything, rest upon unknown laws beyond the control of men. "Things happen because they must happen;" a fatalistic view of history which one finds it difficult to share with him. "War and Peace," aside from its artistic merit, is a great historic picture drawn vividly and impartially, without political bias. It is less valuable, although not less interesting, as a philosophical treatise in which Tolstoy struggles with the old problem of predestination and free will. It is of supreme importance, because Tolstoy discovers for us the mass, the common, unknown, unsung unit, which is moved, not by the will of man, but by that power which we call "Providence." He presses upon the attention of thinking men the new science, sociology. Above all, the book is of interest because all through it is the struggle of a great soul trying to understand the meaning of life. After all the attempts to unravel the tangled web of crossing thoughts, he says, through the lips of Prince Andrey, "Faith is the power of life." When a man lives, he must believe in something. If he did not believe that he must live for something, he would die. Without faith it is impossible for man to live.

One who reads this book for the interesting story which it tells would gladly dispense with its sociology and philosophy; one who considers the work solely from its artistic standpoint finds Tolstoy's views obtrusive, and marring the beauty of the whole; but they belong to the autobiography of the author's soul, and without them the "Life of Tolstoy," which he is writing into every story, would not be complete.

CHAPTER XII

" ANNA KARÉNINA "

ANY man who was concerned about his literary career as such would have continued the writing of historic novels, after the phenomenal success of "War and Peace." Tolstoy, however, was being more and more absorbed by the problem of his own life, and to entangle it again into historic events was much too irksome ; nor did it quite harmonize with his view of the province of his art. He had written a few chapters of the discarded " Decembrists," and had begun to study the life of Peter the Great, in preparation for a story dealing with that period ; but although he gave a whole year to this latter task, he suddenly dropped both subjects and began his "Anna Karénina."

The story has no large historic background, and we are never taken out of the domain of that small world which calls itself by the generic name, "society" ; a domain which Tolstoy now knew better, and loved less than ever. Weak, vacillating creatures they are whom he drew: strong only in maintaining certain worldly standards, and outwardly eager to do the proper thing, while leading a decidedly improper life. He came in touch with them every day: Betsy Tverskaya, who with one hand holds on to the court and with the other digs in the moral mire; Stepan Arkadyevitsch Oblonsky, who believes that the "purpose of education is to get pleasure out of everything," and who manages to do so, in spite of the fact that poor Dolly, his wife, grows prematurely old and wrinkled, and has her life almost ruined because he does not know the meaning of the seventh commandment.

Then there is Vronsky, who falls in love with Anna, the heroine of the story, the wife of a disagreeable but conscientious official. Vronsky has an exaggerated sense of that kind of honor which prevails more or less in all military and aristocratic circles. He believes that he must pay his gambling debts, but that the poor tailor may wait; he believes that it is wrong to cheat at cards, but thinks it perfectly proper to run away with another man's wife. These characters Tolstoy met daily in his social intercourse ; he felt them as influences in his own life, and he struggled against them and conquered them.

The plot of "Anna Karénina" is the simplest possible ; although there are really two stories in one, side by side, and touching each other at many points. The one story is that of Levin, a homely, angular, country-bred aristocrat, who is, nevertheless, thoroughly democratic and feels himself one with the people. To love or not to love them is not a question for him, because he is a part of them ; nor could he criticise the bad or praise the good, because he could draw no contrasts between them and himself. He works with the peasants, eats his bread in the sweat of his brow as they eat, often wondering whether he ought not to throw aside all the past, its inheritance and achievements, and in reality become a peasant. The city is to him a Sodom and Gomorrah, a modern Babylon ; and all his naturalness and buoyancy leave him as he comes in touch with its life. He feels keenly the social lies and insincerities which manifest themselves at calls and balls ; consequently he is not a good conversationalist or courtier. He blushes like a girl when an impure subject is broached ; for he is not half so bad as the young and old men around him. He is in love with Kitty, a beautiful, but in no way an extraordinary girl, whom he adores with a pure and noble passion, and finally marries. They move to his estate, and although the supermundane bliss of which he dreamed does not quite materialize, they "live happily ever after." In great contrast to this natural and idyllic life is that of Anna Karénina, who lives in the world and is of it ; whose husband is cold, exacting, lifeless, and loveless; "for whom the word love would not exist, if it were not in the dictionary." The moral atmosphere which Anna breathes is poisonous, and she has no hold upon anything but her child. She does not love her husband, who is sixteen years older than herself ; religion is absent from her world, and where it is present it is either hypocritically servile or mystical and false. She meets Vronsky, the young cavalier, who has beauty, youth, and strength, but no character; although in his world this last quality is of the least importance. He and Anna seem drawn together by some unseen force, and the newly awakened love is like an uncontrollable fire which burns all bridges behind them. They go abroad together, love each other, and quarrel with each other. Returning to Russia, the ties by which Anna holds him grow weaker; conscious of this and the loss of her position in society, which closes its doors to her, she throws herself under a passing train. She is tempted to this mode of ending her life by the memory of having first met Vronsky at a railroad station, when the maimed body of a workingman was drawn from under the wheels of the engine.

Somewhat in the background, but not indifferently or indefinitely drawn, is the character of Dolly, who is small, wrinkled, pale, and insignificant, between the splendid Anna and the lovely Kitty. In her mended jacket, with her faded hair and complexion, she arouses one's pity as she listens to Anna, who narrates to her the story of her downfall. She is the personification of common, every-day virtue, which "has its own reward" of pain, tears, and poverty. Her husband falls as low as, and lower than, Anna; but, man-like, he has no twinges of conscience, and is unhappy only when, through the discovery of his fall, the household machinery jars. Dolly is a sort of feminine Tolstoy, and his real heroine.

Through a peasant "who lives for his soul and believes in God," Levin discovers the way to the life eternal. Faith saves him and his, and makes his home a center of happiness and a spring of life. On the other side is the home of Anna Karénina, in which there is no love, but only unsatisfied passion ; no thought of the soul and so much thought for the body ; no truth, but every word a deception and a lie ; no true marriage, but what is really only adultery. Such a home has in it the seeds of death ; and such a life, which was lived only for the flesh, must also "of the flesh reap corruption." Levin's soul-life is with but little change taken from Tolstoy's own experience at this stage of his life. Levin's progress from unbelief to belief begins at the deathbed of his brother, and ends when he learns the power of faith and the secret of prayer. Faith comes to him without blinding him as it did Paul, or making him ecstatic as it did Peter, at Pentecost. Faith has not taken away his old happiness, nor has it overwhelmed him by a new one. He does not know whether it is faith or not; but a new power has come into his life, has comforted him and brought him peace. He knows that he will remain a man, a human man with many of his old passions and desires ; he will still be angry with his peasants, and will never be out of the reach of temptation. " I shall never quite understand the meaning of prayer," he says: " but I shall always pray, and my whole life shall be independent of the things which happen to me. I shall live no thoughtless minute as before ; but I shall implant into each moment a positive good."

Although Tolstoy values this story so little, and was very eager to be done "with this tedious Anna Karénina," it marks the height of his artistic power. It is written with much human passion, and in the hands of a man with lower moral ideals and less artistic skill it might have proved dangerous material. It is realistic to the core, because Russian society is realistic ; it has not a trace of Anglo-Saxon prudery, but calls a spade a spade, and does not blush at it or stumble over it. Tolstoy's realism differs from its Russian namesake, imported from France, in being blunt, plain-spoken, and unscented. Sin may be pleasant, but it is never beautiful or harmless ; and any one who reads the motto which he has written over this novel, "Vengeance is mine, saith the Lord," and who understands his plain speech, must know that his realism is as vital as that of the prophets and seers, and that it is not the literary form of decadence. He began the story already knowing the end. From the moment when Anna and Vronsky meet each other with an impure thought which becomes uncontrollable, the reader knows what the end will be. No matter where they are or what they do, whether they meet in secret or openly, whether they go to Italy to study art or return to Russia to improve an estate, whether they eat or drink, ride or dance, the shadow never leaves them, and vengeance is expected ; nor does it delay its coming. Only a very perverted or immature mind can find in any of Tolstoy's stories the slightest encouragement to commit sin.

While "Anna Karénina" was written with much physical vigor, and practically at the prime of Tolstoy's manhood, it was written with the greatest moral passion. He was beginning a new

career and seeking a new purpose for his life.
The faith in God which in the story is still indefinite, was ripening into God-knowledge; and his
search after some solution of the pressing problems was being rewarded by his finding it in the
Gospel of Jesus, whose apostle he was to be,
whose life he was to try to live, and whose precepts he was to teach. "Anna Karénina" was
written at this strategic juncture; and it marks
the parting of the ways and the beginning of
the new life. A story written in such an atmosphere, and which has behind it such moral
struggles, cannot be, and is not in the least,
impure. There are portions of it in which we
should like to soften the realism, and from which
we should be glad to expurgate the seemingly
unnecessary details of which the Anglo-Saxon
does not speak in public; but Tolstoy could not
always stop to clothe naked Russian truth in
English tailor-made words, and we shall have to
read him in unexpurgated editions or not read
him at all. His characters, of which many crowd
the small canvas, are clear, plain, living, every-
day creatures; but always types of social and cultural development. None of them is put there

without a purpose, whether he says or does much
or little. Each one is a symbol of something good
or evil, something to be chosen or avoided. Tolstoy's narrative is as simple as his plot. He never
stops to analyze character, but he describes in the
simplest way the life of a man, never forgetting
the slightest details. He does this with such
frankness and acuteness that the character is revealed from the first moment, and one is never in
doubt "whether it is good, or whether it is evil."

As in "Anna Karénina," so in nearly every one
of his novels, there are really two stories : the one
taken from the life around him, full of varied
human interests, never commonplace, always
highly dramatic, but not theatrical, and full of
poetry which is seldom sweet but always rugged ;
a story which is fiction based upon the experience of others. The other one has all through his
works the same hero, sometimes under one name,
sometimes under another; it tells little of ex-
ternal things, but much of that which happens
within the soul. It is philosophic and didactic
rather than dramatic and poetical, and is not
fiction but history, — the history of Tolstoy. He
does this, not because he feels himself so impor-

tant, but because he desires to know of what value he is to the world, among those others with whom he lives. He knows himself better than any one else knows him. His self-analysis is keen, open, and often seemingly unjust; but unjust only because we are not used to dealing so honestly with ourselves, and because perfectly honest biographies are rare outside of the Bible. As an artist he wrote what he saw in others, and what he experienced through them in mind and heart; as a judge, physician, philosopher, and preacher, he wrote what he saw in himself from his earliest youth; and as he hid nothing from himself so he hid nothing from the public, which was to him not an audience but a judgment hall. So, more and more, the artist gave place to the soul biographer; much to the chagrin of the critics and perhaps of the reading public in general, which always cared more for the story-teller than for the prophet and seer.

CHAPTER XIII

In January, 1881, Countess Tolstoy wrote to her brother: "You would not know Leo, he is so changed; he has become a Christian and he remains one, so steadfast and true." Back of this simple statement of Tolstoy's conversion, for such it must be called, in spite of the fact that the word has become commonplace and almost meaningless in Protestant America, — back of this conversion lie long years of conflict such as few souls have experienced. It was a conflict of spirit which became so painful that it drew the body into its comradeship of suffering, and the whole man was undone. Had Tolstoy been less rationalistic, or had he been born in a climate where the sun burns poetry into each human thought, he would have described the birth of his soul as a miracle, which might have found a place in the traditions of the church and earned him a " handle " for his name and a halo for his head. By his keen, plain, truthful speech, he reveals to us the whole inner process, yet without making it less a miracle, if that may be defined as something which lies out of the ordinary human experience, and which cannot be apprehended by the senses. It is true that during Tolstoy's whole life he had struggles with himself and his surroundings ; but they came at long intervals, and served in no small measure to stimulate his artistic faculty, although they left him spiritually just where he was before. Moscow society accepted his moralizing under the cover of fiction, just as it accepts the fiction which has no cover and no morals. In spite of his love for the peasants, his altruistic schemes, and his pedagogic journal, he had serious lapses into aristocratic Russia, and Prince Obolensky wrote in his memoirs: "Very often I met Count Tolstoy at Peter Samarine's, where there was much society, and where hunts and races were organized. Tolstoy was then (1870) not a philosopher as now, but a jolly enthusiastic sportsman as well as a splendid conversationalist, and his quarrels were always interesting."

The happiness which Tolstoy found in his

marriage did not give him that hold upon life nor the self-control that he expected from it. His passions were not dead, nor was his thirst quenched, nor were his ambitions stilled by the new life, although his wife brought into it all that he could reasonably expect. She loved him as passionately as he loved her, and perhaps less fitfully, after the manner of women; she looked carefully to the ways of her household, and was indeed the ideal of Lemuel's mother: "The heart of her husband doth safely trust in her, so that he shall have no need of spoil." She was economical because Tolstoy never was, and she was ambitious for him because he had ceased to be so. He was more or less swayed by her perfectly human and rational ideals, and in a letter to "Fyett," written in 1873, he speaks of her influence over him. On the eve of his greatest soul struggle he says: "Every day for nearly a whole week I have been sitting for the painter Kramskai, who is doing my portrait for the Treytiokofsky gallery. I have consented to do it because the artist himself came and promised my wife that as a return for the favor he would paint one for us cheaper; and my wife persuaded

Drawn by J. Repin

COUNT LEO TOLSTOY

me." This last phrase does sound as if the story of our first parents were not altogether fictitious; but it is just possible that Tolstoy was not so willing a victim as was Adam. He himself says of that period: "The new conditions in a happy home life drew me away entirely from seeking to find the common purpose of life. My whole being was centered in my wife and children, and for their sakes in care for the enlargement of my means to carry on the increasing household." He was so happy that, "If a good fairy had come down from some strange world and asked me if there were anything I wished for, I could not have thought of anything to ask." Fifteen such years passed, during which his home, his schools, and his new books bade fair to drive away those higher aspirations and silence his questioning soul; yet the inner strife never ceased, for it manifests itself in his writings and in his letters to his friends, which sound much more serious than ever. "You are ill," he writes, " and think of death, but I am well, and must constantly think of it." And again, soon after this: "For the first time you talk to me of God and of divine things; but I have been thinking of these questions for a long time. Don't say that one cannot think about them ; one not only can, but one must. At all times the best men, that is, the true men, have thought about them, and if it can't be done as you say, we must find some way in which it can be done. Have you ever read Pascal? "

A more positive and definite evidence of a coming change appears a little later, when he writes : " Although I love you as you are, I am a little displeased with you because like Martha, 'You are cumbered with much serving' when 'But one thing is necessary.' The mere joy of living is too great in you ; when some day the thread of life threatens to break, it will go hard with you. I have no interest in life, and nothing seems to matter." The question of the purpose of life, to which he had to cling whether he cared to or not, grew slowly to be the all-absorbing one. He says of this time : " Something very strange happened to me. I had moments of great doubt, when life itself seemed to come to a standstill. I did not know how I should live or what I should do. I lost my balance and became melancholy. At first this occurred at long intervals, and I took up old habits again ; then it happened oftener ; but at the time that I finished writing ' Anna Karénina' my despair was so great that I could not do anything but think of the dreadful condition in which I found myself." He sought, asked, and knocked in all directions, and received no answer. " But I must know," he writes. " Before I can trouble myself about my estate or my children or the writing of books, I must know why I do it. Before I know that, I can do nothing ; I cannot live."

The thought of self-destruction came upon him with a strange force, and he had to hide everything which might have suggested suicide. As the sight of a rope roused in him the desire to end his life, so the sight of wife and children made him wish to cling to it. " I tried with all my might to break away from life, just as formerly I endeavored to make my life better." All this came to him in his prime, in the midst of what men call happiness; he was a proud father, the owner of a large estate, and at the zenith of his literary career. He was physically so strong that he could do a day's work in the harvest-field without fatigue ; while mentally he felt himself sound, and able to stay eight or ten hours at his desk. Yet he cared not to exist unless he knew the purpose of his life. He turned from science and from modern culture with a feeling of repulsion; for he felt the inability of the first to solve the really important problems of life, and the hollowness and falseness of the second, if one were honest enough to penetrate its fine veneer. Like a questioning Job he stood before the awful something, uttering his complaint, and the answers of Socrates, Buddha, and Schopenhauer were like the stereotyped phrases of Job's friends, who tried to heal his hurt by commonplace words. Not unlike King Solomon, having tasted of all that the world could give him, Tolstoy cries out: "Vanity of vanities, all is vanity." "What profit hath a man of all his labor which he taketh under the sun? One generation passeth away and another generation cometh, but the earth abideth forever." He turned to the men and women of his acquaintance, studying them carefully to see how they looked upon this question which had brought him to the verge of despair, and he found that they had four ways out of the difficulty. One was the way of ignorance.

They did not know that such a question ever penetrated a human brain; they sipped honey until something called their attention to the bitterness of death, and then they suddenly ceased to sip honey. He could not unlearn what he knew, and consequently could not learn from the ignorant. The second way was that of crushing the question in the pleasures of life. "Eat, drink, and be merry, for to-morrow thou shalt die;" or, in the preacher's words which he quotes: "There is nothing better for a man than that he should eat and drink, and that he should make his soul enjoy good in his labor." The wealth which these people have, the pleasures in which they indulge, bring about a moral torpor which makes them forget that there are such things as sickness, age, or death. The third way was that of suicide; ending life, when one recognizes that it is vanity. This was a way out of the difficulty which Tolstoy at that time thought the most honorable and dignified. The fourth way was that of weakness; to know that life as one understands it is vanity, yet still continuing it, as if waiting for something better, which never comes, and always eating, drinking, and writing books as he was doing. He finds no answer among the men of his class, and yet, he says, there are millions and millions of men who never think that their lives have no purpose, who in contrast to the restlessness of the ruling minority are calm and quiet, who in spite of hardship, hunger, and cold, have a peace of soul and a harmony of spirit which those do not possess who have wealth, knowledge, leisure, and pleasure. Where do they find the power to live and endure? and now Tolstoy finds the answer: "Faith is the power of their lives." Faith is the certainty that human life has a purpose, a certainty through which these human beings live; so he went about seeking it, and was ready to accept any faith which did not ask for the denial of reason: "For that would have been a lie." He studied Buddhism, Mohammedanism, but above all, Christianity, its books and its followers. This study of religions was not a superficial one; it was so thorough that he knew not only their principles, but he caught also the peculiar flavor and poetry of each.

In the study of Christianity he turned first to the people of his own position in society who

were commonly called Christians. He talked
with priests, monks, and theologians of the orthodox and liberal type ; but he found that their
faith had nothing to do with their lives ; that
it was a thing wholly apart, that they clung to it
for one cause or another, but not for the great
reason of finding an answer to the question of
the purpose of life. He also found what he knew
before — that their lives were wholly at variance
with their professions. As he found this among
priests and laymen alike, he turned his attention
to the peasants, in whom he had long suspected
that he would find the real treasure. He stood
on the highway which led past Yasnaya Polyana,
and talked to the pilgrims who went to Kieff or
to Jerusalem. He talked to them as few men of
his station could talk ; he spoke to them like a
brother ; like a child who was going to school
to these other children, the Russian peasantry.
And they talked to him as they would not have
talked to any other nobleman. They looked out of
their frank, open eyes into his, and revealed to
him the secret of their souls, which really was
no secret ; for they revealed it in their lives and
looks.

These people had what he sought—a life in harmony with their faith. "To them life and death are in God's hand, and death is the entrance into life eternal. They do not fear the mice which gnaw at the root to which they cling, and when they lose their hold they go into the depths without a murmur." Tolstoy learned to love and appreciate the peasants more and more, and for two years he prepared himself for the next step; that of ceasing to live like a parasite and of giving his life a meaning, by labor and by faith. He began to seek God, and realized that he failed to find him, not because he was not reasoning right, but because he was living wrong. He knew that there must be a God, although philosophy taught him that one could not prove his existence. He ardently prayed for a vision of that God whom he sought with all his heart, but there was no answer, until one day in the spring-time as he was walking through the woods which surround his estate, and was listening to the music of the awakening life in the tree-tops, this came to him like a revelation: "I can live only when I believe in God; when I do not believe I feel as if I must die. What seek

I further? Without him I cannot live. To know God and to live are the same thing. God is life." Something within him seemed to say: "Live seeking God then, for there is no life without him." "It grew brighter around me and within me, and that light has never left me."

Thus Tolstoy was saved from despair and suicide; and just as gradually as the thought of self-destruction had come, so now came the thought of life, to abide with him forever. And, strange to say, this new faith and this power to live were really not something new, but the old faith and the old power which were in him when as a child he grew conscious of life. It was only a returning to the belief of his childhood — to the belief that the purpose of life was to be in harmony with the Divine Will; but with this difference: that formerly he had felt this unconsciously, while now he knew that he could not live without that trust in God. He compared his condition with that of a boy who was put into a boat, he knew not when or where. Some one showed him the direction of the other shore, put oars into his unskilled hands, and left him alone. He rowed as best he could row, and made some progress, but the farther he went, the stronger became the current, which carried him far away from that other shore. Around him he found in increasing numbers those who, like him, were being carried away by the current. Some were throwing away the oars in despair, some struggled against the stream, others again, drifted along. The farther he rowed the more he forgot the shore which had been pointed out to him, until at last he let go of the oars in utter hopelessness. The jolly crews of surrounding boats assured him that their way was the only right one ; and he, believing, rowed with them until he heard the roar of the rapids and saw the destruction of their boats. Suddenly, in his agony, he remembered the other bank and pulled back to it, although the wind was against him. " The shore was God, and the oars were the liberty given me to find my way back to the shore and be with God."

With all the zeal of a convert who finds the truth late in life, he turns to the Church, prays devoutly, fasts as often as is decreed, goes to confession, and takes Holy Communion. But soon new doubts creep in, and as might have been foreseen, his questioning mind cannot be silenced, and, "Why do I do this?" and, "Why do I do that?" he hears ringing in his ears at every service which he attends. The forms, which in the Greek Church are so numerous and so seemingly stupid, repel him because they have no vital connection with life, and the oft-recurring holydays have no meaning. They celebrated things which he could not believe; another matter which made him stumble was, that the Church was then praying for the victory of the Russian army over the Turks. He asked himself : " How can one do that when Christ says, 'Love your enemies'?" Again he thought of those words, when Alexander III. ascended the throne with vengeance in his heart against his father's murderers. Tolstoy interceded for them in the name of Christ; nevertheless they were executed, and their death was approved by the Church and its priests. New doubts arose as he came to study Church history. So many churches, so many claims to infallibility ; and how difficult it was to say which was right and which was wrong. He said : " All of them contain truth and falsehood, but I must find the truth." He searches the Scriptures, in which all profess to believe, he studies them ardently ; and like Luther he finds the truth in the Gospels, which he recognizes as the source of all life. As he studies these Gospels, a new vista opens before him, and he sees the Kingdom of God, which is so different from the kingdoms of this world, political and ecclesiastical.

The call into this Kingdom, which comes to him unmistakably and clearly, he immediately obeys. Like the disciples who "left their nets and followed him," he was ready to leave everything he possessed — more valuable indeed than fish-nets and boats. To him, to know means to obey ; to believe means to live ; and obediently he conforms to the teachings of Jesus as he interprets them. His money he will give to the poor, his life is to be the simplest, his bread is to be earned by the sweat of his face ; and if the art which he forsakes again presses the pen into his hand, it shall be consecrated to the preaching of that truth which put meaning and value into the life which was so meaningless and valueless that he was ready to throw it away.

CHAPTER XIV

THE story of Tolstoy's conversion was carried into all corners of the earth and into strata of society which had never known of him as an author, or realized the moral import of his stories. It seemed that the world had been waiting for a man who would not only interpret the Gospel rationally, but live it radically ; and Yasnaya Polyana at once became a new holy shrine to which pilgrims from afar came by the hundreds. Letters poured in upon Tolstoy in such numbers that it was found possible to answer only comparatively few. Many of those who crowded around him at that time came because, like him, they had puzzled over the great question of life, and desired to hear from his own lips how it was answered. Others, burdened by their sins, came to repent, and others again came with strange heartaches to find here their relief. Many of those who went to him found, after doing farm labor for a few days, that sore muscles would not heal sore hearts, and that carrying water from the pond did not lift burdens from the conscience. So they returned to the world which they had left, with mixed feelings toward the physician whom they could not help admiring, but whose medicine they found too strong.

A very small but important minority remained to labor, and after leaving Tolstoy, took up life even more severely than he was living it. Among them were Prince Chilykoff, who sacrificed his millions, Vladimir Tshertkoff and Paul Biryukoff, who are living in exile on account of their avowed Tolstoyan tendencies, and who in Geneva and London are publishing Russian newspapers, whose spirit is in harmony with the teaching of their master. Beside these there were numbers of the nameless ones who were "destitute, afflicted, tormented, and of whom the world was not worthy." Most interesting is the fact that, like a new Messiah, he drew to himself a large number of thinking Jews, some of whom organized communities according to his principles. One of these is that of Mr. Femerman and Mr. Butkyevitch, in the district of Cherson, in southern Russia. Others, emulating Tolstoy's example, forsook their bartering to begin tilling the soil; and the best Jewish colony in Palestine was recruited from Jewish university students of Odessa and Moscow, who were "Tolstoy mad," as they expressed it. The Jews came to Yasnaya in goodly numbers to see a man who was really living the Christian life, not merely preaching it; and under the influence of that life they accepted the Christian faith. At first Tolstoy encouraged the baptizing of one or two of them into the Greek Church; but he always expresses himself as regretting this act. If he had had Jewish blood in his veins, he would have found it difficult to prevent his being declared the Jewish Messiah. As it is, he has been the first Russian who has interpreted Christianity to the Jew in terms which he could accept, and in a form that has nothing of the idolatry of the Greek Church, which is the greatest barrier to the Jew's acceptance of the Christian religion. Tolstoy was besieged by over-anxious mothers, who accused him of bringing pressure to bear upon their sons, who had developed the "Tolstoy disease"; and he and all his followers were considered ripe for the lunatic asylum. It even happened that in some instances men who returned to their estates, to live according to Tolstoy's teachings, were declared insane, while others were sent to prison and into exile. But Tolstoy was neither the organizer of a movement nor a zealous propagandist. He did not care whether he had followers or not; and when men and women came to worship him, he would say in the language of the Angel of the Apocalypse, "See thou do it not, — worship God;" and when they called him Master, he said: "One is your Master, even Christ." When they called him Teacher, he answered: "Call no man Rabbi." He did preach to every man who came; if he were rich he took him into the woods and looked into his soul with his piercing but kindly eyes, saying repeatedly and insistently: "Sell all thou hast and give to the poor." When the mighty and strong came and asked what to do to be saved, he would tell them: "Thou shalt not kill." When the spiritually blind came he repeated Christ's words: "Blessed are the pure in heart, for they shall see God."

TOLSTOY THE MAN

To the Socialists, with their grievances and schemes, Tolstoy said : "For man shall not live by bread alone." He was indeed a "Gospel Preacher," so narrow that he saw salvation in nothing but in the teachings of Jesus, and so broad that he saw salvation for all who followed the Christ, no matter to what church they belonged, or whether they belonged to any. While he did not shrink from accepting the consequences of his teachings for himself, he did not force others to do so, and to a friend who found it difficult to part from his land he writes thus : "Do not mind what the world will say about your retaining your property ; it is a question which concerns you alone ; and if your conscience does not condemn you, do just as you have planned."

In his family circle he was tolerant, allowing each member of it the fullest liberty. Only two of his children believed as he believed, but after a while they also, like so many others, found the path too rugged, and "thenceforth they walked no more with him." Strangers came and offered him their wealth and their services, but he always warned them against too hasty action, and never accepted their money, while more than once he sent men back into their former callings. He could also quickly detect the motive which brought men to him, and would startle them by his keen perception. When a man came burdened by a great sorrow, and offered himself for some service without having consciously revealed the cause of his coming, Tolstoy said to him: "Go home, and after your great sorrow has spent itself, come again." A young Russian teacher, repelled by his vocation and inspired by Tolstoy ideals, came to him, and he generously said : "Go back to your desk, you are doing more good than I am." Every one who came, he received graciously, and although his time was more than fully occupied, he gave of it unstintingly to all who asked for it.

The writer of this volume remembers his first pilgrimage to him, as a young, enthusiastic student, who had suffered spiritual shipwreck, and saw in Tolstoy the refuge and the harbor. He will never forget how this man, who himself had struggled through, listened to the unripe thoughts of a boy who could scarcely express himself — one who, when he began to speak, hardly knew just why he had come there. In common with others, he felt the magic of that personality which loosened the emotions ; but which held one's tongue the tighter. No priest ever received more honest confession than Tolstoy received ; for lying in his presence was an impossibility. Many men after a first conversation have come back and said: " I am sorry, but I have not told the whole truth." Some people have been repelled by him, but they were those who went to him as they might have gone to the Pyramids, the battlefield of Waterloo, or to some wonderful freak museum. Rude he never was, although many a time his visitors were as inconsiderate of him as they are of historic places; and only his being very much alive saved him from being carried away bodily by relic hunters.

It is true that in Yasnaya Polyana the curious had much to see which seemed not a little queer to them. Here was a man steeped in the culture of his time, wealthy and highly talented, yet wearing a peasant's coat and doing a peasant's work. They laughed not a little when they caught a glimpse of this intellectual giant mending his shoes, when, as they argued, he might have made much money, or created some work of art with those fingers which drew the waxed thread so unskillfully through an old shoe which was not worth the mending. They did not realize that this laborer Count, this shoemaker author, was trying to mend a rent in human society as well as the rent in his shoes. From afar they watched him, as by a mighty effort he followed his peasants, cutting rye and oats, "eating his bread in the sweat of his face" under the trees which edge the village fields; and they said: "What a foolish thing for a man to do, — a man who might grace any society by his presence, enhance its pleasure by his conversation, or influence men by his thoughts." They little realized that this man was cutting a swath like that of the giant reaper of whom the peasants tell; who leveled forests by one sweep of his mighty scythe. Tolstoy was followed by other reapers, and will still be followed in those fields ripe for the harvest. Each autumn will bring men nearer to the golden days of the Kingdom of God. He was himself unconscious of the power of his example, nor did he realize the oddity of his position. He was not "playing to the galleries," to use the phrase of the street; he was not playing at all; he was simply living his faith with an unconscious intensity. His rugged face, with its mixture of peasant and noble, received a new and strange expression. Its strength became suffused by tenderness, and none could look into that countenance without being conscious not only of the man's sanity but also of his sanctity. Seeing him, one lost all thought of the strangeness of his position; for everything blended with his nature harmoniously. It was the harmony which follows a great struggle; it was not stagnation, for the man was still full of vital thoughts, and the strength of his body, mind, and soul seemed inexhaustible, making one feel the influence of that power.

If the crowds which gathered in Yasnaya Polyana had been asked, "What went ye out for to see?" or, "What have ye seen?" they could have given no intelligent answer. They saw a man who, like the Baptist, was not clothed in soft raiment, yet in those earlier days one could scarcely escape the thought that the peasant's garb which he wore was very becoming, and that he knew it. He was homely, like the heroes of all his stories; the face was angular, the features

were unmodeled and sharp, but the whole gave
the impression of great force. He was a piece of
original material in which all the possibilities
of human nature lodged in their fullness. One
realized that he could have been as cold and cruel
as Napoleon, or as warm and kindly as Abraham
Lincoln; and that in him dwelt the spirit of the
finest aristocrat beside that of the commonest
mujik. The spirits of war and of self-sacrifice, of
lust and of the highest purity, of deceit and of the
greatest truthfulness, of extremest pride and of
lowliest humility, mingled in him, and have made
his heart their battle-ground. One had the impression that although one had seen faces which
resembled his among Russian aristocrats and
peasants, one had never met just such a man.
He was a composite photograph of Russian society, in which his own self came to the fullest
expression. Just as Russian society lacked the
middle class, so the feeling for that class seemed
in him to be utterly lacking. The physician, the
mechanic, the lawyer, the merchant, and all the
other products of modern development found in
him no sympathizer, and little by little dropped
out of the list of his visitors.

TOLSTOY THE MAN

Those who came were divided by the Tolstoy family into three classes. The first class was small; composed of those who, like Prince Chilyoff, Tshertkoff, and Biryukoff, were Tolstoyans in thought and action. It is doubtful that of this class one could count more than the apostolic number, of which a few were women; notably among them one with a very uncommon name in Russia, — Mrs. Smith, who lives close to Yasnaya Polyana, in an exalted poverty, echoing every thought of Tolstoy; herself the personification of simple-minded goodness. Among the un- known, one would have to name Mr. Nyikitoff in Moscow, who not only stepped from wealth into poverty, but who also drew the members of his family into his condition, not without dire consequences to them. One of the sons, upon being deprived of his money, shot himself, and the remainder of the household became estranged from its head, who is living in one room in ex- tremest poverty, yet feels rich in the conscious- ness that he is obeying the law of Jesus. He is one of the most perfect examples of the thor- ough Tolstoyan, outranking his master in many respects. Among these might be counted a num-

ber of men who were Tolstoyans before Tolstoy ;
leaders in the numerous sects in which Russia
abounds, and who not only learned from Tolstoy,
but also left some valuable lessons behind them.
They were welcome visitors, and Tolstoy's indebt-
edness to such men as Sutayeff, an uneducated
peasant, and Bondareff, a Siberian exile of the
same class, cannot be definitely estimated. There
were also numbers of men who, by the reading
of the New Testament, had come to strange
thoughts, which led them away from the
Church, and who, hearing of Tolstoy, clung to
him as the expression of their unexpressed ideas,
henceforth enrolling themselves among his
disciples. There are not a few of these among
Moscow's wealthy merchants ; and Tolstoy's
friends always find his name an " Open sesame "
to their homes and their life's story. Among
these are such men as Petrovitsch, Vulganoff,
and Dunayeff, well-known bankers, all of them
splendid examples of a Christian manhood which
is as rare as it is beautiful. To the second class
belong the many who came, saw, and heard, and
returned to their homes with a new influence in
their lives but unable to sever themselves from

the wealth and culture they possessed, or the society in which they moved. Among this class must be named all the painters and sculptors for whom he sat, and who could not loose themselves from the wholesome spell which he cast over them. Of these Ilya Rèpin, Ossip Pasternak, and Prince Trubezkoy are the best examples. Their homes and their lives are permeated by his spirit, their art is influenced by his teachings, and they are the disciples "who walk afar off." America enrolls among this class Ernest Howard Crosby, one of the best loved visitors to the Tolstoy home. His worth can be best estimated by the fact that he has been able to cast a halo over many other American tourists who came, who were hard to get rid of, who had much money, much tactlessness, and that perseverance which is not the "perseverance of the saints." Jane Addams, of the Hull House in Chicago, the best type of American womanhood that ever stepped into the Tolstoy home, came, carrying with her the fragrance of her devoted life. In spite of the fact that Tolstoy was then on the verge of a long illness, and not in the best spirits, she had that delicate perception which saw the genuine man and his great and struggling soul. She was only a few hours in Yasnaya Polyana, and her name may have been lost in the long list of those who came from all the corners of the earth, and who returned blest, and henceforth to be a blessing. Of these no record has been kept; but after all they may have been the best mediums for the spreading of Tolstoy's ideals and the multiplying of the divine life upon the earth.

To the third class are consigned all those who place Tolstoy among the "things" which must be "done while one is in Europe;" the newspaper reporters who magnified themselves and their subject, and who searched for queerer things than they found; the men and women who called themselves "saviors of society," the apostles of new dispensations who came to convert Tolstoy to every possible and impossible faith, and who returned disappointed because, while they found him non-resistant, he was not non-committal. All were welcomed, some more cordially than others. Those who needed help, and for whom help was good, received it; and most of them went away with the feeling "that it was good for us to have been here," although many mocked and ridiculed what they could not understand.

The one element which more or less mars the great impression one receives is the fact that there are two worlds in one household, and that the world in which Tolstoy lives is invaded at every step, making it incomplete. His plain rooms are joined by those of his family, almost luxuriously furnished ; the frugal kasha (gruel) which he eats is surrounded by omelettes and porterhouse steaks; and this man who desires to be like one of the commonest peasants sits at a table served by white-gloved lackeys. He is poor, it is true ; he has no money in his pockets, but his sons have it. They married rich wives and enjoy " an abundance of the things which men possess." He does not accept money for his writings, he throws them out into the world; but his wife gathers them up, until the income from them reaches into the tens of thousands.

Tolstoy cannot be blamed ; for he had no right to force his family to live as he lived ; nor can one blame Countess Tolstoy, upon whom the burden of the family rested, who was eager to clothe and educate her children according to their station in life, and who with much labor succeeded in doing so. The matter did not pass into this stage without a severe struggle, and that she was the victor in it need not prove that it was really the woman through whose fault Paradise was lost. Yet every one feels the presence of these two worlds, — the one reserved, cautious, pleasure-loving ; the other simple, generous, full of labor and sorrow ; and if any chance guests were asked in which world they would rather spend the remainder of their days, most of them would say : " In the world of labor and poverty." There is a lesson in the contrast. One sees those who are of the world, and close to them him who is in their world but not of it ; and when one goes away, he takes with him the full spiritual charm of that peace which pervades in such abundant measure the life of Tolstoy.

CHAPTER XV

IN the year 1883, Turgenieff, from Paris, where he lay upon his deathbed, wrote to Tolstoy imploring him to return to the art from which he had fled to become a preacher of the Gospel of Jesus, and a prophet of the Kingdom of God. Turgenieff wrote : "I have not written to you for a very long time because I have been very ill, and am now lying on my deathbed. I shall never recover ; I know that positively. I write to you purposely to tell you how glad I am to have been your contemporary, and to ask of you the granting of a last wish. Do return to your art. The gift you possess comes from the same source from which all good things proceed. How happy should I be if you would listen to me and grant my request. My friend, great writer of Russia, do listen to me ! Let me hear from you when you receive this letter, and let me embrace you and your family once more."

Neither the plea of the dying nor of the living friends could persuade Tolstoy to take up his pen for any other purpose than that of proclaiming the truths he had discovered concerning life, and doing it in a plain, straightforward way, without the cover of fiction. He wrote now as ever from within and of himself ; and in writing obeyed that ever-present desire for confession and self-examination, more than the desire to impart knowledge to others. In his first didactic book, "What is my Faith?" he describes how he has come to his faith in Jesus and in that portion of the Gospels which he believes to have proceeded from the lips of Christ, and which has revolutionized his own life, bringing him peace and happiness. The center of his faith and of the Christian religion he finds in the Sermon on the Mount to which, he says, the Church pays little heed, being too much occupied in proclaiming fasts and feasts, and explaining strange doctrines and dogmas. The doctrine of non-resistance seems to him the most important, and becomes the text of all the sermons which he preaches to individuals, authorities, and nations. Over and over again he says : "Force must never be used, even in the suppression of evil, and wrong can effectually be righted by repaying evil with good." He discovered in the Sermon on the Mount five laws which have become his rule for faith and conduct, and which he believes will bring the Kingdom of God into men's hearts, and peace and happiness upon the earth. The five laws he summarizes thus : —

"Live at peace with all men and do not regard any one as your inferior."

"Do not make the beauty of the body an occasion for lust."

"Every man should have only one wife and every woman only one husband, and they should not be divorced for any reason."

"Do not revenge yourself and do not punish because you think yourself insulted or hurt. Suffer all wrong, and do not repay evil with evil ; for you are all children of one Father."

"Never break the peace in the name of patriotism."

These five laws, which overlap one another and are not very clearly defined, represent the great principles upon which Tolstoy would base the new world order. To the question, how a state or society can exist without the use of force, he gives the following answer, which is characteristic, inasmuch as it is the answer which he always gives when one questions his theories. "There can be no answer to such a question," he says, "because the question is wrongly put. We have nothing to do with the organization of the state or of what we call society, but we have everything to do with the question how personally we have to act in the face of the ever-recurring dilemmas; whether we are to subordinate our conscience to the conditions around us, or whether we are to feel ourselves at one with a state which hangs erring people to the gallows, which commands soldiers to commit murder, and poisons and demoralizes people with alcohol and opium, or whether we are to subordinate our actions to our conscience alone, so that consequently we cannot have any part in the actions of the government which offends our conscience. What form the state will have, what results such actions will bring, I do not know. I know only that if I follow the promptings of a reasonable love, the results cannot be evil; just as nothing evil can happen when the bee follows its higher

instincts and goes with the swarm to its destruction. Herein is the power of the teachings
of Jesus : that they bring one from a condition of
doubt to a position of absolute certainty. I wish
to repeat it," he says, "the question is not, What
form of government is the safest? but the one
question for every man, and a question which one
cannot avoid, is whether a good and reasonable
being who has come into the world for a brief
moment and at any moment may disappear from
it, — whether he can be a party to the killing of
erring people, or to the killing of all people without exception, who belong to a different race or
nation and whom he calls enemies. There can be
only one answer to the question, What the consequences will be. I answer, only good ; for only
good can come if we act according to the highest known laws, according to conscience and
love." If one replies that to live according to
these laws one has to suffer, he says : "And don't
they suffer here, who do not live according to
these laws? Just walk through the streets of
your cities and see these pale, emaciated creatures who struggle for their daily bread. They
have left house and home, wife and children for

the sake of a living, and yet they are not satisfied; neither the poor devil with his hundred rubles, nor the rich man with his hundred thousand rubles. These are the true sufferers. They lack all conditions of happiness. They lack first of all the touch with nature; they never see the sun rise ; they see forest and field only from their carriages ; they have never sown anything, and like the prisoners who find comfort in a spider or a mouse, so these people find comfort in parrots, dogs, monkeys, or sickly plants, which often they do not even attend to themselves. Secondly, they lack that happiness which labor brings ; first, pleasant and voluntary labor, and then physical labor which brings sound sleep and a good appetite. All the unhappy ones of earth, dignitaries and millionaires, like prisoners have no work ; and they struggle against diseases which are a result of this lack. Only such labor as is useful and pleasant makes happiness ; and as these people need nothing, their labor is always distasteful to them ; for I have never known one who praised his work, or did it with the zest with which a porter shovels snow from the sidewalk. The third condition of happiness which they lack is the family. Most of the worldly minded are adulterers; and where this is not the case children become to them a burden rather than a pleasure. If they care for them they do not associate with them. They are left in charge of strangers; first, foreign governesses and tutors, and then the officials in the schools; consequently they have from their children only sorrow; that is, they have children who are just as unhappy as they are, and who have only one feeling towards their parents; namely, the wish that they may soon die, so that they may inherit their wealth. They lack the fourth condition of happiness; the loving association with people of all stations and conditions; for the higher a man rises in life, the narrower grows the circle with which acquaintance is possible. The peasant may associate with the whole world, and if 1,000,000 people refuse to associate with him there are still left 80,000,000 who live and work just as he does and with whom he may come into immediate relationship, whether they live in Archangel or Astrachan; and he need not wait for an introduction, or make formal calls. The fifth condition of happiness which they lack is health and a painless death; and the higher the social standing the more do they lack these conditions. Take the average well-to-do man and his wife," Tolstoy continues, "and take a peasant and his wife and compare them, and you will find that in spite of the hunger which the peasants endure, and the cruelly hard work which they have to do, they are usually the healthier. Call to mind the majority of rich men and their wives, and you will find that the greater number is ill. Think how most of your rich acquaintances have died one after the other of some loathsome or terrible disease. They ruin themselves for the sake of the teachings of this world, and countless men and women follow them, living the same cruel life and dying the same painful death. And shall we not go, when Christ calls, to the obedience of his law?" To the criticism that his teaching would immediately result in poverty, he replies: "Yes indeed, but what does it mean to be poor? To be poor means not to live in the city, but in the country; not to be locked up in a room, but to be at work in field or forest; to rejoice in the beauty of the sky and the warmth of the sun. To be poor

ENTRANCE TO YASNAYA POLYANA

means to be hungry three times a day, to sleep restfully instead of having insomnia; it means to have children and to train them yourself; it means to be able to associate with most men; and above all it means not to have to do that which is distasteful to you, and not to fear what is to happen. Jesus said: 'The laborer is worthy of his hire,' and he who works will get enough to eat. Moreover, we are not in the world to be served but to be of service to others. Thus the true happiness and the true wealth will come if we obey the law of Jesus."

Two purely theological works follow this confession of his faith. One of them is a "Critique of Dogmatic Theology," and the other a translation of the four Gospels, which he has woven into one. In the first work it is the theology of the Greek Church that he makes the target of an unusually sharp and bitter attack. He says: "It grows clearer to me every day that for some reason it seemed necessary, at the expense of healthful reasoning, and the laws of logic and of conscience, to reduce God to a low, half-heathenish conception. . . . The whole teaching of that church is not only false, but a lie and a deception, which for centuries has been built up for certain base purposes." He closes the book very sarcastically, citing the last sentence from the "Simple Theology" of the Church, where it teaches that "He who rules the universe has appointed the earthly rulers, and has given them dominion and power for the well-being of the people; moreover, that God through these rulers appoints all lower officials," and this sentence ends in an admonition "to be regular and faithful in the payment of taxes and tithings." To this Tolstoy adds these words : "With this moral application of Christian dogma, ends the 'Simple Theology.'" In a later work upon a similar subject, he is more outspoken, and characterizes theology as "An infamous tool of politics." The relation of theology and politics, or of the church and state, he describes thus : "Rome was, at the time of the rise of Christianity, a nest of thieves which enlarged itself constantly by robbery, and which subjected other nations by force and murder. These robbers with their leaders, who were now called Cæsar and now Augustus, plundered and murdered people in order to satisfy their fickle desires. One of the heirs of these robber chiefs, Constantine, came to the conclusion that certain Christian doctrines were preferable to his own ; perhaps the following : 'You know that the princes of this world have dominion over them, but it shall not be so with you.' 'Thou shalt not kill, thou shalt not commit adultery, thou shalt gather treasures upon the earth, judge not, resist not the evil.' Some one must have told Constantine something like this : 'You want to call yourself a Christian, and at the same time disobey these laws, continue to be a robber chief, to go to war, to live in luxury, and to kill. Well, all that can be reconciled.' So the Christians blessed Constantine and praised his power and influence, they declared him the chosen of God, and anointed him with holy oil. As often as a rascal succeeded in robbing, plundering and killing thousands of people who never did him any harm, they anointed him with holy oil ; for of course this was a man of God. As often as one of these 'anointed of the Lord' had the desire to beat his own or a strange people, the Church prepared holy water for him. They sprinkled with it the cross, — that cross which Christ carried and on which he died because he resolutely condemned these murderers, — the priests took it into their hands, blessed this man and then sent him out to murder and to hang in the name of the crucified Christ." Tolstoy is generous enough to say that the priests were corrupted by these robber politicians, and that only later did they become conscious and professional deceivers. The relation of church and state he defines thus: "The words 'Christian State' have about as much meaning as 'hot ice,' or 'glowing ice.'" There is to him only one alternative: "Either there is no Christianity or there is no State."

Thus Tolstoy proves himself an anarchist, and he does not hesitate to call himself one. "Do not be afraid of that word," he said to the writer, "I am such an anarchist as the early Christians were ; I am such an anarchist as the words of Jesus have made me, and by-and-by we shall become accustomed to the true meaning of that word. The man who is born again needs no civil or military authority, and it can have no power over him." Little as Tolstoy's Christian anarchy can have any relation to the ordinary state, just so little relation has it to what we understand by anarchy, which we define as "A system which teaches that an ideal condition of society can be brought about by revolutionary force." Neither is it in any way related to modern socialism, whose theorizing he considers as false as the conclusions which it draws. The ideal society which Tolstoy preaches cannot be brought about by any of these agencies, but rather by the influence of those individuals who live according to the law of Jesus.

His translation of the Gospels is accompanied by quotations from Russian and foreign commentators, with whom he discusses the meaning of the text. Beside the Greek text, he printed the Russian translation, and finally his own ; always stating the reason for his deviation from the Russian. This large work he condensed into a smaller one, leaving out his comments and those of the commentators. Arbitrarily he divides the Gospels into twelve parts, and he proves his division by citations from the words of Jesus. Each chapter is headed by a quotation from the Lord's Prayer, which is the briefest expression of what Jesus meant to convey by the words which follow. He has left out most of the miracles as well

as everything which was not quite clear to him;
and the following narrative of the sick man at
the pool of Bethesda, characterizes his whole
treatment of the Gospel story. "In Jerusalem
there was a bath, and a sick man was lying
there — without making an effort, expecting to
be healed by a miracle. Jesus stepped up to the
sick man and said: 'Do not expect healing
through a miracle, but live according to the
strength which is in you and do not deceive
yourself about the meaning of life.' The sick
man obeyed Jesus, arose and went away." In
spite of many such liberties with the text, the
work startles one by its ingenious compilation
as well as by the skill with which Tolstoy makes
the words of Jesus conform to his ideas. The
best known among his didactic works he calls,
"What shall we do then?" Only small portions
of it have been printed in Russia, and abroad it
has appeared in a somewhat incomplete and mutilated form. After having been away from the
city for more than eighteen years, he tells of
his first touch with its life, and especially with
that part of it which hides itself in the cellars
of Moscow and in its wretched asylums and

slums. He came in close touch with it during his services as a census enumerator ; a work which he undertook in order to be able to make investigations in regard to the prevailing poverty, and to find ways and means for its prevention and relief. He tells how he came to one of the most wretched of these places, the Rhasonoff Asylum. Something very wonderful happened to him there. He had taken money with him and could not rid himself of it, although he had brought it with him for that purpose. "For," he says, "I met there in those cellars people whom I could not help because they were used to hardship and labor and had a stronger grasp upon life than I had. Again I met others whom I could not help because they were just such people as I was. The majority of the unfortunates were unfortunate merely because they had lost the ability and the desire to earn their daily bread ; that is, their misfortune consisted in the fact that they were just as I was. Real suffering was relieved in these places by their own comrades, better than I could have relieved it. Money could make none of them happy." He comes to the conclusion that poverty can be

stopped only as one goes to the root of the
evil; and the evil is our whole social fabric.
"What shall we do then?" he asks. "Do just
what Jesus and John the Baptist told us to do.
Give up everything which we do not absolutely need, and adjust our lives so that we will
have to take as little as possible of labor and
strength from others. There is no such thing,"
he says, "as a privileged idle class, although we
have been trying to prove that the division of
labor necessitates that some shall paint and
think while others perspire and labor. We call
painting and thinking, art and science; but art
is art only as it conveys to men the highest idea
of life and salvation, and science is truly science
only as it teaches men what is their object in
life and what their destiny. We call that, con-
temptuously, religion; but it is the only true
science. Counting invisible bugs and stars, looking for sun-spots and moon channels, and add-
ing to it an 'ology,' does not make a true science;
and upon such science and such art we cannot
base our unjust social division." He insists
that the so-called scientists misunderstand Christianity, that they judge it from the distorted

faith of the churches, and that they take less trouble to probe for the genuine faith than they do to search for the history of the pollywog. "What shall we do then?" he asks again; and answers : "Let us not deceive ourselves as to the meaning of life; and as soon as we realize that we are upon the wrong path, turn about and walk upon the narrow one. Secondly, let us not believe that we are better than others ; and, lastly, let us work with all our might physically, and struggle with the forces of nature for the maintenance of our own lives and the lives of others."

"What is the purpose of life?" he asks in a book which is as didactic as the others, but much more sweet-spirited ; and he gives the answer in one sentence : "The whole aim of life is self-sacrificing labor for others."

That Christianity is not a mystical religion but a new philosophy of life, he declares, and proves in his most important work of this kind, "The Kingdom of God is within you." It is an enlargement of his first work, "Confession of Faith," and here he searchingly reviews all his teachings, and tries to prove them. He points to the Church as the enemy and perverter of Christianity, and warns men not to judge it by that institution, meaning primarily the Greek Russian Church.

There are, according to Tolstoy, three ways of looking at life. The first and oldest is the individual or animal, which considers the preservation and well-being of the self, regardless of the consequences to others. All the heathen religions in their perverted forms teach this, as do also Buddhism, Mohammedanism, and even Christianity. He considers this stage the childhood of the religious consciousness. The second view of the aim of life consists, not in the well-being of the individual, but in that of a number of individuals — such as the family, a tribe, a nation, a state, or humanity as a whole. From this view have developed all patriarchal and social religious faiths ; such as the Chinese, the Japanese, the Jewish, the state religion of the Romans, and our own state religion as well as the so-called humanitarian religions like the Positivists. " The third view, which is represented by Tolstoy, and over and over emphasized in his teachings, is, that the purpose of life is not in the attaining of the well-being of the individual, or of any class or number of individuals, but to express and to serve that divine will which has called forth the whole earth; or, as he states it less technically, "It is the business of every man 'to do the will of Him that sent me into the world.'"

Humanity, he claims, has passed through the first two stages, and now is the time to begin the fulfillment of the third, which begins by accepting the law of Jesus. To the criticism that this ideal is unattainable he answers that "it is our business to try, and that in trying there will be an increase of the well-being of all. The time will come," he says, "when what seems to us impossible and visionary, will be perfectly natural and easy to realize. The world is now suffering from the discord between conscience and action. We still rule over men, and consider them our menials and servants, in spite of the fact that our conscience tells us that all men are equal. We obey laws which are human, imperfect, and unjust, we go to war and murder men, we smother conscience by narcotics and luxuries, by music, art, theatres, smoke, and alcohol. Nothing can save us from this inconsistency and struggle but the Christian faith as expressed in the law of Jesus."

This constant attack upon our view of the aim of life has not remained without its effect upon individuals of all classes, and has reached from the mujik's cabin to the throne of the august czar. The proposal of the Hague Conference for the settlement of international difficulties, which emanated from the czar, is one of the tangible results of Tolstoy's ungentle and insistent teaching. Another result is a deeper look into the meaning of the Gospels on the part of the Church authorities in Russia ; a more humane treatment of prisoners and a greater philanthropic activity among the rich in the cities of Russia ; the last improvement being due largely to Tolstoy's condemnation of wealth, its use and abuse.

Again let me say that his teachings come from within the man as they have been borne in upon him from what he thinks is the will of God and what he sees of the suffering of men. He felt the great contrasts which in Russian cities are stronger than elsewhere; he saw flaunting luxury and pitiable poverty side by side, and he cried out against such conditions, which are in

Photograph by M. Duumpilbr

COUNT TOLSTOY AND HIS DISCIPLE AND FOLLOWER
THERKOW

discord with the will of a loving God. No one will ever know how these harsh sayings of his were born out of love for man, — for the common man ; the suffering and patient mujik who supports a vast state by his labor, receiving in return scorn and abuse, and enduring hunger and cold. Tolstoy has idealized the common man ; but no more than has the Master who held up a little child as a model to pattern after, and the self-sacrificing gift of an outcast woman as the most fragrant of offerings ; passing by kings and priests, to call the fishermen of Galilee to be his apostles and disciples. Tolstoy dignifies labor, physical labor, and calls all of us who live by our brains, "social parasites." He may be wrong ; but after all has been said, it remains true that the man who gives, in exchange for the bread he gets, the exertion of his muscle and the sweat of his brow, is the most honest man. In a country like Russia, where to live off the state is the business of a good third of its population, and where common labor and the common laborer are regarded as both " common and unclean," his condemnation may be a just one if not always temperate.

He exalts the words of Jesus, and condemns

the Church which has made of a religion, pure,
lofty, and spiritual, one of signs, wonders, idols,
and forms. Neither is the exaltation too high or
the condemnation too severe. The words of Jesus
are life, while the mumbled words of Russian
priests are like the enchantments of sorcerers
and soothsayers, and have deadened the spiritual
life of their adherents. Tolstoy does not claim
that his teachings are original. "If they were
original," he said to the writer, "they would not
be true." The truth he teaches is as old as all
truth; it was born in the bosom of God before
the world was, and brought to light and into life
by Jesus Christ. Nor are Tolstoy's teachings pro-
found; he means to be so simple that a child
can understand, and it is his desire for simplicity, that garb of truth, which made him for-
sake an art into whose atmosphere he was born,
which wooed him in his youth, which, in middle
age brought him far-reaching fame, and in the
winter of his life never-fading laurels. He
shrank from nobody and from nothing when he
felt it his duty to say just what he thought to be
the truth, and what he knew to be the will of God ;
for he had not only the teacher's insight into truth,

but also the prophet's courage and the seer's vision of God. The Czar's throne was not so high to him as the throne of God, the Metropolitan of Moscow not so sacred as his divine Master. Both were condemned, and were called murderers and idolaters. He was excommunicated, and he would have been imprisoned or exiled if these powers had not realized that he was not fighting with carnal weapons, and that they could not defeat or silence him by chains or dungeon walls. It is a case where a man has proved true the words of the prophets, and the common teaching of history, that "Out of the mouth of babes and sucklings," and not out of the mouths of mighty guns, or mightier kings, "Hath he ordained strength."

Tolstoy has opposed the hard and cold dogmatism of the church, and has put into its place the reasonable and broad teaching of Jesus. He denies the existence of a God who is man-made, whimsical, autocratic, and arbitrary, and believes in a God who has revealed himself in love and law, and who permeates all things. He denies the efficacy of punishment in the redemption of men, and the use of force in maintaining or defending states, nations, or society ; and teaches that men who voluntarily obey the law of Jesus, will alone bring the Kingdom of God upon the earth and establish it. He denies that patriotism is a virtue, and that killing men in battle is not murder; he teaches that all men, of whatever race or color, are brothers, and that the law of Jesus which bids us to love all men must be obeyed, rather than the dictates of earthly authorities, which force us to carry arms and use them either in the defense of old, or in the acquisition of new territory. Neither hate nor vengeance should have a place in human hearts, he says; and men will be redeemed, and society redeemed, only by the divine pity and loving forgiveness.

Whether he be right or wrong, he is so sure of being right that he has placed his whole life in the balance; believing that he knows the truth, and that it is the truth of which Jesus said: "It shall make men free."

CHAPTER XVI

THE MISUNDERSTOOD TOLSTOY

DURING the winter of 1903, while recovering from a severe illness, Tolstoy received a letter from an English friend, calling his attention to the fact that Louise of Tuscany, the divorced wife of the Crown Prince of Saxony, had excused her action in leaving her husband and children by saying that Tolstoy, through his teachings about matrimony, had encouraged her deplorable action. This letter, which he answered in a somewhat ungentle spirit, a fact which he afterwards greatly regretted, pained him very much ; for he, in common with all great teachers, was realizing that many of his precepts, although he tried to make them very plain, had not only been misunderstood but also misapplied. Especially was this true in regard to that very subject of marriage ; a relation which he *maintained purely and sacredly,* and against whose abuse and misuse, particularly in the higher circles, he had lifted up his voice. The "Kreutzer Sonata," the book in which he presents his views of matrimony among certain classes, created a great sensation in Russia and out of it, and is certainly the most misunderstood, and consequently the most unfortunate of his writings. His idea of literature, which made him write so plainly that "he who runs may read," has had just the opposite effect from what he intended ; for they who ran away, misread and misunderstood him, and made him the apostle of libertinism. Although he tried to prove that without a true view of life, and without noble ideals, even matrimony may become immoral, many, if not most people understood him to mean that matrimony is no better than concubinage, or, perhaps more correctly speaking, that concubinage is as good as matrimony. He tried to show that marriage does not save a man from committing adultery, even with his own wife ; but men and women understood him to say that there may be unlawful relations between the sexes without committing adultery. His own view of marriage he expressed to the writer in these words : "Marriage is an elevation for such as we." He considers that much which happens

in the married life is a lowering of that state,
which he does not consider the ideal one, but natural and sacred. Basing his views upon the words
of Jesus in Matt. v. 28, and xix. 11, 12, he considers the single life the ideal one, even if so the
whole human race ceases to exist. Upon no other
point does one meet so many criticisms and condemnations of Tolstoy and his views as upon this
one ; and he is especially censured for not living
according to what he teaches to be the ideal married state. While he would not defend himself
against these, one can truthfully say that as soon
as he had light upon the subject he took what he
considers the first steps leading to the ideal; steps
which he believes it possible and essential for
every man to take. The first one, "purity before
marriage," he did not attain because it was never
held up to him as an ideal; adultery in the single
state with a lewd or a married woman being not
only uncondemned but encouraged. Tolstoy confesses his unconscious sin in this, and has long believed that impure relations, at any time and in
any state, are absolutely sinful and against the law
of Jesus. He says that the second attainable step
is "the maintenance of the married state with

one woman." He has met this requirement in the face of a society which encouraged the coveting of another man's wife, and where the temptations to break this law were many and great, both from without and from within. No one will question the fact that he has been faithful to his wife, giving her his fullest devotion and purest love. The children who were born to him were not unwelcome to Countess Tolstoy, in whom the mother spirit is remarkably developed, and who believes with her husband that the aim of marriage should be to give to the world well-born and well-trained children. She believes with him that the children should not be given over to the care of strangers ; she has nursed all but one of them herself, and was much grieved that she could not be to this child a mother in the fullest sense. Tolstoy also believes that it is wrong for a woman to use her physical charms to attract men to herself, and he therefore condemns many of the usages of polite society. In the "Kreutzer Sonata," he means to show to young people, first, the evil of sensual passion ; and, secondly, how the married life may be debased by that passion. He does this with his usual candor, thus making the story exceedingly naturalistic, and consequently unpleasant ; perhaps unwholesome ; but he certainly is not and does not wish to be impure.

Nor does he attack the family ; on the contrary, he has always been its strongest champion, and intends to be that in this much misunderstood book. The story is told by one Posnyscheff to his traveling companion in the railroad car. It is the sad history of his courtship and marriage and their unhappy ending. He had tasted life after the manner of young men, and was finally lured into matrimony by a designing young girl who used her physical charms to great advantage. They were married, but never knew real happiness, because they were drawn toward each other by only the lowest desires, and were quickly separated when these desires were satisfied. Their children were unwelcome, and were not trained by the parents, but left to the care of hirelings. A musician, who came into the house as a friend, charmed the wife by his good looks, but more by his playing on the violin, and at last by his ardent professions of love. The jealousy in Posnyscheff's breast grew from suspicion into

madness ; and one night, returning from a journey (which he had undertaken solely to be able
to surprise his wife with her paramour), he killed
him, was imprisoned, and had time to repent of
his deed as well as of matrimony. He was convinced that, if he had had as much light upon the
subject before as he had then, he would never
have married; and he realized that Christ's words,
"Whosoever looketh on a woman to lust after
her," have their bearing not only upon the wife
of another man, but upon one's own wife also.
Tolstoy does not prove by this story that matrimony is a failure, but that the men and women
who enter it without the highest ideals before
them, make a failure of it, and are no better, and
sometimes worse, after they are married, than
they were before.

Countess Tolstoy and her children were not
pleased by the book, because it was natural that
the public should in some way try to connect the
story with the author's life, which, in other cases,
it was quite justified in doing. Tolstoy is anything
but unhappy in his married life, and Countess
Tolstoy anything but an impure woman ; nevertheless, he writes out of his own experience when

he speaks of the base effects of passion upon the higher life. He entered the married state as he would have entered Paradise ; and he deplored the fact that he brought into it so much which defiled and destroyed its sacredness as well as its purity. In the " Kreutzer Sonata " he did not say all he wished to upon this subject, although many people think he said too much. However that may be, it must be remembered that everything he did say he said seriously, and with the simple desire to tell the truth as he saw it, and was trying to live it. He certainly did not give any encouragement to the libertine, or the free-lover, or any of those sentimentalists whose soaring emotions may be only the stirring of the baser passions. He believes in the marriage of the heart ; by which he means that marriage which so unites two souls that no power on earth can separate them. None of those men and women who have broken the chains of wedlock, and have run away from its responsibilities, no matter how galling and heavy they have been, can find a syllable in all his teachings to encourage them. His standard for the married life is the standard of Jesus, as he interprets it, and is much higher than that of the state and of most of the churches. He would condemn the action of those who break the marriage vow, if he did not believe the words of his Teacher: "Judge not, that ye be not judged." It is the fashion to sneer at Tolstoy's theory of the higher wedded life, because his wife has borne him thirteen children; but if they were born out of a pure love, as we have every reason to believe that they were, he has fulfilled the first condition which he has marked out as one of the steps towards his ideal. Perhaps he felt the non-married state to be the perfect one, because in it one can more easily live as he himself desired to live. "Happy man!" he said of a confirmed old bachelor; "he can live without hurting anybody." Marriage and the children have kept Tolstoy from making of himself the completest sacrifice, and testing to its extreme the truth of the law of Jesus. He still thinks the martyr's death desirable, and now, with neither wife nor children dependent upon him, he would deem it his greatest joy to suffer thus. He did consider his family, — he had to in order to be consistent; for he could not force any one to live as he wished to live. His ideal — undesirable, or unattainable, as it is — has this advantage, that the steps which he marks out toward reaching it are both desirable and possible, and are the greatest need of our modern society.

Tolstoy's attitude toward women lacks all the sentimentality by which he surrounds the peasant. He is a realist in their portraiture, although it never lacks the human touch which he gives to everything. The "woman question," as such, has no place in his social problems, because under the law of Jesus "there is neither male nor female;" the least is as the highest, and every one is a servant to his fellow men. Upon women in the new spheres of activity, he looks with the same disapproval as upon men in similar positions; contending that those occupations are unwholesome and unnecessary.

Another matter upon which he has been misunderstood is his view of art. In the "Kreutzer Sonata," and later, in his "What is Art?" he attacks the sensuality of art, but not art itself, which he loves in all its forms. All through his life he has felt its seductive power, and its ability to be made a tool for the lowest instincts; its capability of filling a man's soul until there is room for nothing else, and the possibility of its becoming his prayer, temple, and divinity. He also attacks its exclusiveness, its expensiveness, and its lack of usefulness in the service of the Master. The art in which he believes must be able to convey the highest emotions to those who come in contact with it ; these feelings must not be superficial, base, or vague, and they must serve to bring men into harmony one with another. Art must be simple in form and clear in expression ; so that it needs no commentary or interpreter. It must be the instrument which conveys moral and religious truth from the realm of the mind to that of the heart, and must bring men in touch with the higher life. By this standard he condemns the music of Wagner, Beethoven's "Ninth Symphony," and Goethe's "Faust" ; approving the folk-song of the peasant, the Old Testament stories, Schiller's youthful tragedy "The Robbers," Victor Hugo's "Les Misérables," Dickens's novels as a whole, Harriet Beecher Stowe's "Uncle Tom's Cabin," and many others of the same class. Just as honestly as he has dealt with his life and condemned it in the light of the truth which he found later, just so he condemns the art which he produced that has not these standards ; and as he has changed his method of living, he has also changed his aim and method as an artist.

It is not such a barren world into which he has escaped and would have the believers in Christ's law to follow. His own home, Yasnaya Polyana, is full of music, not always that which he desires ; but men and women bring to him the best they have, and he enjoys all that finds its way to his heart. The silent rooms have often been filled by the sweet, pure notes of Mozart, his favorite composer, whose masterpieces he plays himself, with the feeling and touch of an artist. Whenever Tolstoy came to Moscow, he could be found, on Sundays and feast-days, in the "Maiden Field," the pleasure-ground of the common people, whose unbounded delight he shared, and in the natural outpouring of whose simple art he found the type for its highest expression. During these winters he often attended the concerts of the Symphony Or-chestra, given in the magnificent rooms of the "Aristocratic Club," and he never hesitated to acknowledge himself fearfully bored ; especially if Wagner dominated the programme, as has frequently happened in late years. Although his own room is devoid of ornament, pictures and sculpture are not banished from his home, and he looks at both in unfeigned enjoyment. Painters and sculptors belong to the circle of his most intimate friends; they bring the product of chisel and brush for his approval, and his criticisms are always listened to reverently, although they are not always accepted.

Nearly everything which the world prints finds its way to his study, and he reads much, or has the substance of the books told to him, by some member of his family. Towards the new Russian literature he does not feel very sympathetic, although it was inspired by him. He deplores its sensuality and its aimlessness, but above all, its lack of truthfulness. And this is after all his greatest test of art: Is it true? Does it truthfully reflect what men feel, think, and do, or what they ought to feel, think, and do? The form of art is of little importance to him; it must be sacrificed to truth. For this reason he prefers prose to poetry, without, however, remaining untouched by the true masterpieces of verse. The writer has seen him moved to tears by the recital of the simple Russian poetry, and has also seen him enter sympathetically into the intricate art of Browning. He himself says upon this subject : " An author is of value and of use to us in the measure in which he reveals to us the inner processes of his soul. Whatever he writes, be it a drama, a learned thesis, a philosophical discussion, a criticism, or a satire, it is the revelation of the labor of his soul which is valuable, and not the architectural form by which he reveals it, or very often tries to conceal it."

Toward the stage he never felt very sympathetic. In his younger years, when he lived a life of pleasure, the play was only one of the means of making it more enjoyable ; but later, life as it was seemed tragic enough, without needing an expensive, and what he thought an immoral institution to represent it. Very sarcastically he describes a rehearsal which he attended somewhere, and which served to separate him still more widely from the stage. He says : " It seems impossible to view a more disgusting spectacle than this. Everywhere there were workingmen, dirty, tired, and in bad humor. On the stage were hundreds of painted and strangely garbed men and scantily dressed women. In the opera which they rehearsed there came a procession of Hindoos escorting a bride. She was led by an individual dressed like a Turk, who opened his mouth in a strange way, and sang: 'I lead the bride, I lead the bride.' Things never seemed to run smoothly; sometimes the Hindoos with their spears came too late, sometimes too soon; seldom in time. Then something happened which made the director swear like a cab-driver. Over and over again the Turk sang: 'I lead the bride.' Once more the Hindoos came, with their glittering spears, and again things were not right, and again there were curses, and again the Turk began: 'I lead the bride.' Such a rehearsal lasts five or six hours; the beating with a cane, the repetitions, the corrections of singers and orchestra, the processions and dances, all of it is well seasoned by terrible oaths. Forty times, at least, I heard the words donkey, fool, idiot, and hag, which were applied to singers and musicians alike; and all of them listened patiently, and marched again and again, and danced over and over, and the Turk sang

for the fortieth time, 'I lead the bride.' The
director knows that these people are so ruined
that they are not fit for any other thing but to
blow a horn or to march over the stage like
fools, scantily dressed, with spears and yellow
slippers; but he also knows that they enjoy this
lazy life, and would rather bear anything than
to leave it, and seek a more honest way of making a living." Not a much less repulsive feeling
was engendered in Tolstoy when listening to one
of Wagner's operas; and he went away vowing
not to attend another performance. He was
nearly sixty years of age when he began to realize that he might use the stage for the con-
veyance of his teachings. Especially during the
now often repeated attacks of illness did he seriously think of writing a drama. He saw the characters acting the play before him; and, judging
from the production, it must have been a decidedly unpleasant experience. Never before has
Russian peasant life been painted in such absolutely black colors; and perhaps there is no drama
in existence which surpasses his in describing
the base in human nature. In his first play, the
sub-title, "When the Claw is in the Trap, the

Whole Bird is soon lost," gives a clearer idea of the moral import of it than "The Power of Darkness," the name by which we know the play. It is taken entirely from peasant life, which is portrayed with marvelous fidelity. The mujik is not in the least idealized, and we see him in all his coarseness, crudeness, ignorance, superstition, and brutality. Nikita, the hero, steps from one sin into the other ; he seduces the orphan Marina, and casts her from him most cruelly, because she is poor. He betrays his master, the peasant Pyotr, with whose wife he has entered into unlawful relations, and he helps her to put her husband out of the way by poisoning him. Then they marry, after which he drinks to excess, and neglects her for her step-daughter, whose relations with him do not remain without consequences. The darkness into which all the characters wrap themselves becomes gruesome ; and the murder of the newly born infant renders the situation unendurable. While its wail is still in the air, its mother is about to be married to a lad, with whom this union has been arranged, without his knowing the dishonor and crime which are attached to her and her family. Nikita's conscience, however, awakens; he leaves the merry wedding guests, and in the barn attempts to commit suicide. His wife and mother, who have been his accomplices, and who are both weak and bad, find him, and chide him for not making ready to go to the church, where the marriage ceremony is to take place. Finding him obstinate, they threaten him; but before all the wedding guests, he falls upon his knees, and, encouraged by his father, " makes a clean breast " of the matter, and goes to prison with a light heart. Those who read the play in the translation, or see it enacted on a foreign stage, lose much of its spirit and its truly Russian flavor. For instance, on the Russian stage, when the woman comes in to get a cross to put upon the child's neck before it is murdered, the audience feels her chief sin, which is hypocrisy, and Tolstoy makes his point; but upon a foreign stage, this act invariably creates merriment, which certainly it was not meant to do. Dark and dreadful as the drama is, it meets the requirement of Tolstoy's ideas of art, and tries to speak powerfully to both the emotions and the conscience. For the women in the play, who are worse than the men, he finds this apology, uttered by the old servant, Nitrisch: "There are millions and millions of you women and girls, and you are all like the beasts of the forest. You grow up and die, and see nothing and hear nothing; you know nothing of God, and you are like blind dogs, crawling along on your way." The men see and know something; they go to town and to the inn, and they come in touch with life, poor as it may be. As a pathetic picture of the condition of the Russian peasant, this play surpasses anything which Tolstoy has written. It is repellent when one reads it, and becomes positively disgusting when seen on the stage. It destroys the idea of the essential goodness of simple people, who are supposed to be spoiled only as they are touched by modern culture; for these peasants, far away from everything which is modern, surpass in brutality and absolute viciousness all that we know of such characteristics among civilized people.

A play which is a keen satire upon society, and in which Tolstoy contrasts the life of the common people with that of the so-called educated classes, was written shortly after this drama ; and those who accuse him of a lack of humor ought to see a Russian audience convulsed by laughter at its presentation. In the play, which is called "The Fruits of Modern Culture," peasants come to town to buy a piece of land from their lord. They are astonished by everything they see and cannot quite comprehend all its meaning. The count is deep in spiritualism, and sees and hears ghosts everywhere. His wife, who has been told that diphtheria is epidemic in the village from which the peasants come, has the room in which they are disinfected by ill-smelling drugs. The poor mujiks cannot understand how they can be full of insects which they themselves cannot see. The daughter of their lord hammers the piano all day. The son belongs to various clubs and societies, and is now especially interested in the "Society for the Culture of Long-haired Greyhounds." The peasants hear in astonishment that the lady has herself tightly laced each day, that her dog wears a costly coat in winter, and that he gets a specially prepared cutlet for each meal.

Unfortunately, the satire is too sharp, and the caricature too broad ; but the play delights

Russian audiences, without making much impression upon those persons who partake of these peculiar "fruits of culture." It was given before the czar in Zarskoye Selo, his summer residence; the different characters were represented by members of the royal household, and the audience was composed of the very people at whom the author's sharpest arrows were aimed.

A third play, written shortly after this one, is called "The Whisky Distiller," and is much less a play than a tract against the manufacture of liquor and the use of it; as such it has been a very great help in Russian society of all classes. As literary productions, all of Tolstoy's plays are inferior to any other form of his writings, and one feels that he has come to the drama too late in life. He has never been in sympathetic relation with the stage and its actors, or with anything that is connected with the presentation of the drama. His aversion to it is best illustrated by his offhand judgment of the "Passion Play" at Oberammergau. The writer came to Yasnaya Polyana, from the Bavarian Mountains, where he had been much uplifted by seeing it. "What can there be beautiful about it?" Tolstoy said, rather sharply. "I should not care to see a fat peasant hanging on a cross. I should think it rather repulsive." And the narrator was checked in his enthusiastic description.

CHAPTER XVII

TURGENIEFF'S wish, that Tolstoy should return
to the art which he had forsaken, was to be fulfilled. Gradually he worked his way back to its
height, through his shorter stories; such as "The
Death of Ivan Ilyitsch," "Walk in the Light,
while ye have the Light," and so, to his last great
work, "The Resurrection." The first of these
sketches is that of a simple and common every-
day life; yet it is a terrible tragedy which takes
place in the conscience of the man, as he begins
to feel approaching decay and death. With marvelous skill Tolstoy pictures the emotions in his
breast, from the moment when his apprehensions
begin until they end in despair. The lies which
are told to the man by his physician, as well as
by the members of his family, add greatly to his
torture, which is not eased until a simple peasant
boy tells him the truth: "We must all die, Mas-

ter." His whole life passes in review before him, and realizing that it was wrong, he repents, the fear of death leaves him as he bravely faces it, and, "in place of death there was light."

The second story, which is the only one in which Tolstoy reaches far back into history for his plot, is that of two men living at the time of Trajan: Pamphilius, who becomes a Christian, and finds in the law of Jesus the happiness of his life; and Julius, his friend, who is of the world, and suffers disappointment after disappointment, in his business, in his own life, and in the life of his son. Crushed by adversity, he seeks Pamphilius, accepts Christianity, lives twenty happy years, and passes into eternity without fearing death when it comes upon him. Tolstoy's own feelings had much to do with the theme of these stories; for old age had crept upon him, and he had more than once faced the great inevitable end. "What does it mean," he writes at this time, "that life is going? That the hair falls out, the teeth decay, and the face is covered by wrinkles? — Everything grows ugly and terrible, while the things I once loved, I abhor. There must be a beauty of real life, a beauty which cannot thus fade away." Countess Tolstoy also writes at this time that her husband is growing gray, that he is much changed, and that he is quite silent. Those who had not seen him for a decade noticed all this; but also realized that in spite of the wrinkled face and gray hair, he had gained a new beauty. The features, so unsymmetrical and roughly hewn, were smoothed over by tenderness; the gray eyes were less piercing and kindlier; for the effect of his new life was written upon his countenance. There was also about him, what one had always missed; that certain something which we call a spiritual atmosphere. He was weaker physically; but there was still a mental power which was remarkable, and was to manifest itself in his "Resurrection," a story which shows all the virility of his youth, surprising his friends and dismaying his enemies. Never before, in the history of Russian letters, had it happened that an author was permitted to print in a journal which had about two hundred thousand readers, a story which so unmercifully condemned the fundamental ideas of Church and State as did this one of Tolstoy. It seemed as if the censor had been hypnotized; because the story, even as it finally passed his scrutinizing eyes, had in it all that Tolstoy said about the farce which is played in Russian courts in the name of Justice, and his dangerous theory of giving all the land to the peasantry. In fact, the government traced certain revolts to these ideas, which had gone among the peasants; and when they were asked why they had rebelled, they replied : "Tolstoy said that the land belongs to us."

Prince Dimitry Necklyudoff is, again, the hero of the story. In the home of his aunt he meets Katyuska, a charming girl, who is something between a servant and a daughter of the house, and whom he loves in an innocent way, she reciprocating his affection. After a number of years, he returns as an officer and man of the world, whose heart and soul have been spoiled, and ruins Katyuska, forgetting her as soon as duty calls him into the service. She is driven from the house as soon as his aunt becomes aware of the consequences of his affection, and sinks lower and lower, until she becomes an inmate of a brothel. Being suspected of having poisoned a rich merchant, she is arrested, brought before the court, and sentenced to banishment. Necklyudoff, her betrayer, is chairman of the jury. Recognizing her, he becomes conscious of his guilt, and tries to make reparation. He wishes to marry her, and offers to share her punishment; but she is deaf to his entreaties, and incapable of reciprocating the noble feeling which prompts him to make this self-sacrificing offer. Slowly, by enduring with her the privations of the prison, and by helping and protecting the many victims of Russian injustice, he is able to awaken in her sparks of her first, noble love. In vain he appeals from court to court, and, finally, to the senate, to have her sentence revoked; and after exhausting all the means at his command, he prepares to go with Katyuska to Siberia. He divides his land among his serfs, and clad in rough, peasant garb, traveling third-class on the railway, he discovers a new world; the world of the honest, hard-working mujik. He follows Katyuska from one prison station to another, and at last is able to present to her the pardon granted by the czar. An exile and prisoner, like herself, a rather remarkable man, has offered to marry Katyuska, who accepts him, knowing that Necklyudoff's life would be ruined if she permitted him to chain it to hers.

COUNTESS TOLSTOY AND THE YOUNGER CHILDREN

He knows that she loves him, and that she is making this sacrifice because of the purity of her affections; although she has tried to hide from him the real cause of her decision. Returning to his hotel, he is burdened by thoughts of the evil he has seen in the prisons during his journey through Siberia. He turns to his New Testament, which was given him by an Englishman who was visiting the convicts, and, in reading it, is filled by the thought that he must not judge, but have the forgiving spirit, even toward those who had so cruelly treated him and his companions. Finally, the words of Jesus, "Seek ye first the Kingdom of God and His righteousness," convince him of the false philosophy of his life, and he determines to seek that which alone can be found. With that night began his new life; "because everything which happened to him after this had a better and a higher meaning."

Both the hero and the heroine have their resurrection. He, from a meaningless and sinful life in the higher circles to a repentance which tried to make immediate and definite reparation, and finally, to true life through his obedience to the words of Jesus. The heroine had her resurrection, from a low and base life, into which she had fallen through the guilt of another, to noble feelings which she had long forgotten, and to which she was awakened by the same man's kindliness and gentleness. The story shows how powerful, still, when Tolstoy wrote it, were his artistic as well as his critical faculties. With what gigantic strength he tore away the covering of modern society! How he probed the wounds of Church and State, until banishment was threatened, and excommunication pronounced upon him! With what childlike joy he draws in the beauties of the spring, and with what prophetic insight he shows the discord among men! Like a John the Baptist, he lays the ax "to the root of the tree;" but with the gentleness of his great Master he preaches pity and compassion for the poor, love and faith, as forces for the redemption of men. It is, no doubt, his noblest story; and were it not that he went so far down for his material, using it without gloss, it might have been one of the finest productions of modern literature. His pity for those who suffer through the guilt of others is as great as his hate for their oppressors, and as is his contempt for their self-sufficiency and complacency. The language in this story is, if possible, clearer and more definite than in any of his other works. There is not a wasted word; the aim is direct and sure, and the reader immediately becomes conscious of the fact that he is in touch with one who is not a mere story-teller. There is no playing with certain theories and maxims; but almost a violent outcry, exposing the lowest depths of human nature, the most hidden secrets of society, and calling men to a "Resurrection," through a pure, devoted, self-sacrificing, and simple life. Tolstoy was very sad and unhappy when he wrote certain parts of this story; he felt himself insulted in his innermost being by the common sins of uncommon men. At the same time he knew that he was once like them. He saw the nobility of men in most ignoble circumstances; in their dirt and degradation, behind thick prison walls, and even in the lowest brothels. That he told the truth, no one doubts and no one has denied. The Russian courts and the Russian prisons are just what he says they are; for he did not get his material from hearsay, or from the Imperial

Library, as is the custom of those who praise in books and lectures Russia's humane treatment of prisoners. He went to the prisons himself; and no one will ever quite know how far he went, — not to get material for his story, but to come near to his brothers and sisters, and if possible make some reparation for his own sins.

What pleased him most after the publication of the "Resurrection," was first, and above all, its moral effect. From nearly every European city came letters from men who cried out: "We are sinners," and who asked the way to their "resurrection." It was the writer's privilege to come with such messages from Vienna and Buda-Pesth, two of the worst cities in Europe, in which numbers of men said to him: "Tell Tolstoy that we shall never again think so ill of women as we have thought." His face brightened when these words were repeated to him; and in them he found his true reward. "Resurrection" was the first book which for many years he had written for revenue, and that not for himself, but for the unfortunate Duchoborz, who had left their native land and had found a home in the far northwest of Canada. His intervention, and the proceeds of this story, saved hundreds of people from being exterminated by the Russian government, and from starving to death upon the cold plains of the Province of Manitoba. Tolstoy refused all other aid so freely offered him for these unfortunates ; preferring to throw them upon their own resources, to save them from what he considered a greater evil : the evil of pauperism.

He did not cease to be a preacher and teacher, because he had written another great story ; for with the echoes of its success still in his ears, he began writing an indictment against the modern movement of Social Democracy, which was published under the title, "Modern Slavery." The writer was in Yasnaya Polyana while it was being written, and had its theories practiced on him during those walks which are so dear to all who visit there. On one of those evenings, as he and Tolstoy were watching the setting sun, the writer, having spoken of his own faith in a future life, ventured to ask : "Count, what about the future? I mean the future of humanity. What will be the ultimate form of society?" "The future," he answered, "is with God to know, and for us to prepare. Our business is to live right, now, and God will make all things right, then." His remark about socialism was startling. "The greatest enemy to humanity is this Social Democracy; it is the preparation for a new slavery. It teaches a future good, without a present betterment. It promises golden streets, without the bloody Gethsemane." "But isn't socialism a preparation for an ideal state?" "No, indeed not. It is just the contrary. It will regulate everything, put everything under law, it will destroy the individual, it will enslave him. Socialism begins at the wrong end. You cannot organize anything until you have individuals; you are making chaos out of cosmos; you will breed terrorism and confusion, which only brute force will be able to quell. Socialism begins to regulate the world away from itself. *You must make yourself right, before the world around you can be made right.* No matter how wrongly the world deals with you, if you are right the world will not harm you and you may bring it to your way of thinking. The modern labor leader wishes to liberate the masses, while he himself is a slave." A few weeks before this, Tolstoy had received a deputation of workingmen from the neighboring city of Tula; men who had become infected by socialistic ideas, and he preached the same sermon to them. They went away much discouraged, but not convinced of the error of their ways. It was not easy to leave him, unconvinced; for while he spoke, his eyes rested firmly upon one, and his sentences came unbroken, like water from a flowing spring. His sermon, for such it always was, awakened in one the consciousness, the holiness, and the responsibility of the self. He magnified the value of the soul, and minimized the value of the things of which the socialists had spoken; the lack of comforts and luxuries. He felt all the wrong which they were suffering, but he insisted that they themselves must be right, "be born again." How often these words resounded among the towering oaks which shade his customary walk. "You must deny yourself, — give up, — renounce, — sacrifice, — and obey only the Christ." To all the philosophy which one quoted, he would say abruptly, "That is not the law of Jesus." He would never grow angry; but he spoke firmly, like one who was convinced that he alone had the truth. At that time he also wrote an open letter on the subject of patriotism, and addressed to the czar. He sent it to a Moscow paper for publication, but of course it was promptly returned, and was afterwards published in London. It elaborates his well-known theory of the evil of so-called patriotism, condemns the killing of countless numbers of men at the command of the czar, and, not in unkind language, calls his majesty a murderer; not less a murderer than the men who, crazed by some fantastic idea, lift their hands against a king, and slay him.

Tolstoy's fame was beginning to reach the masses, among whom discontent had manifested itself, and they were looking to him as the champion of their rights. The following letter which he received is interesting, because it testifies to this growing feeling, and because it graphically and truthfully pictures the condition of the peasantry : —

Most Gracious Sir, our defender and protector :
We kneel before you, weeping hot and bitter tears, and pray that you may not leave us ; even

as a father does not leave his children. We want
to tell you how the authorities are treating those
of us who have become Sectarians. The police
of the whole district have come, and they go
at night from one house to another, cursing, and
frightening the women and children. Wherever
there was a soul which had cut itself loose from
the Church, there the police came, and settled
down, often six or eight of them, and ate and
drank. They asked for eggs, milk, and butter,
but paid for nothing. The housewife had to
serve them, and stand before them while they
were eating. They beat old women who were
too feeble to wait upon them. They asked for
horse and wagon, and if any one refused, he was
beaten most unmercifully. The Sectarians were
driven out of one village by the other inhabitants, because of the continued persecution on
the part of the authorities. The peasants who
wanted to help these persecuted people were
themselves persecuted and fined.

We pray that a man may be found who could
tell our woe with such a loud voice that it might
be heard in Heaven; because we cannot do it
ourselves. They press our throats, so that we

cannot even talk in a whisper. Letters are not sent to us, or from us, and we are completely isolated from the world. The officials have grown so violent that after the czar had pardoned eleven women, they refused to sell them railroad tickets at Charkoff; so they had to walk, carrying their little children in their arms. After twenty miles, they succumbed; and only through the intervention of a charitable woman did they finally get transportation to their homes. If only some one would help us, who are suffering such great misfortunes!—some one who would be led by the Spirit, and who could fly like a bird through the whole world, and proclaim to it our great woe.

The world did hear; but not the Russian world, for its ears and eyes were closed by the censor; and the peasants who wrote this letter suffered severely; for it is still forbidden in Russia to complain audibly. Tolstoy's fame as a champion of the people's rights, and as their helper in need, dates from his remarkable effort in their behalf, when in the year 1891–92, he was the leading spirit in relieving the distress caused by the famine. Money and helpers came to him from all parts of Europe and America; and his leadership was as successful in this philanthropic movement as had been his reluctance to undertake it. He traveled, in the depth of winter, from village to village, organizing relief societies, and establishing soup-kitchens, which were the means of keeping millions of peasants from starvation. The closing winter of the nineteenth century Tolstoy spent in the Crimea, carried there because of his severe illness; his friends hoping much for him from the mild climate of Russia's Riviera. There he lived again his eventful youth. His literary career seemed past, his health was failing, and although the fine climate permitted him to recuperate to some extent, he returned to Yasnaya Polyana the next spring, an old man, who was waiting for " one fight more; the best and the last."

CHAPTER XVIII

TOLSTOY THE MAN

SOME time ago one of the most widely circulated German journals sent requests to its readers to name the most celebrated ten living men. Tolstoy was given the first place by hundreds of votes; and there was scarcely a list sent in from which his name was omitted. The same thing, it is reported, was done in France with very much the same result. This kind of tribunal may be worth much or little, nevertheless it indicates the fact that among living men there is none whose name is more widely known than that of Tolstoy. His books have been translated into all the languages spoken among civilized people; and a recent and somewhat inaccurate compilation of the books and articles to be classed under "Tolstoyana," numbers more than four thousand. Of course the number of books written by him and about him indicates nothing beyond the fact that he is a voluminous writer, and that he has aroused much critical comment among men. He is known beyond the reach of his writings, among millions of peasants who cannot read ; and among countless numbers of all classes who have never had the opportunity or taste to read anything that he has written. Into the obscurest corners of the earth has his fame gone, and one is startled by seeing how instantly his name awakens interest and provokes comment and discussion. To some, he is, like Isaiah, a great prophet who has again brought to men the first true notes of religion ; or a John the Baptist, the forerunner of a new kingdom. To others again he is the veritable Anti-Christ; his teachings destructive of Christianity and void of what they call true religion. Some, again, consider him a man, half lunatic, who has perverted his art and misused his grand opportunity of giving to the world great novels ; while others talk of him as a shrewd *poseur*, who has increased the sale of his books by studied oddities and eccentricities. But no matter what men call him, they all agree that he is a wonderful personality whose influence has permeated civilized society; and even his severest critics have felt this influence although they may have

studiously avoided reading his books. It seems
as if great thoughts become an atmosphere which
men must breathe in, whether they choose to do
so or not; and in spite of themselves they begin
to think those thoughts even if they do not immediately act upon them. Tolstoy's feelings or
something like them have come to many an officer in the Russian army, who had fought, gambled, and drunk, and who suddenly asked himself:
" Have I been doing right ? " and some evening
he would communicate his thoughts to a companion, swearing him to secrecy, and he would
reply: "I have been thinking the same thing;
this is not life, this is death; " and the next day
they would resign their commissions and be
declared "Tolstoy mad" because they began to
earn their bread by the sweat of their brows.
Many a judge who arrogantly meted out so-
called justice to his fellow men, saw a " hand-
writing on the wall:" "Judge not that ye be not
judged," and stepped from his bench, among the
culprits. Legislators and officials in our own
country have felt this influence in a similar way ;
and at least one place, the city of Toledo, is governed by a mayor who acknowledges himself

Tolstoy's disciple. Little villages are named, of whose existence he does not even know, in which households are governed by the law of Jesus ; and the number of wealthy manufacturers who have been influenced by him in the treatment of their employees is larger than one would imagine. Among many he is a "fad," which however cannot endure, because Tolstoy can never become fashionable ; and you cannot put his teachings on and off like a garment. They grip the life as by a mighty force, and no matter how much one shakes one's head over them, and how much one lives in direct opposition to them, one can never quite shake off the feeling that, after all, the inner life is of more value than mere adventure, and the inner joy more than what men call happiness ; and while most of us say we cannot live like Tolstoy, nearly all of us wish that we might. One would scarcely have thought that so serious, so religious a literature as Tolstoy has given us could gain any foothold, especially in Europe ; which was under the sway of German rationalism and French naturalism and from whose sphere Christianity in its severe aspects was quite ruled out ; and yet Europe has not been so dominated at any time since literature has been an art which touches more or less all sorts and conditions of men, as it is by the writings of Tolstoy. In Russia as well as in other countries of Europe, men talk about the ethics of Jesus as they have never talked before; and they do it largely under the influence of this great personality. Peter Rosegger, who in the Austrian Alps preaches a sane and sweet religion, and who lives close to the people from whose loins he sprang, says: "All modern, social, and spiritual movements, even such as do not wish it, are coming near to the Christian ideal. To live for others, to see in the well-being of others one's own happiness, to help the weak and downtrodden, to forgive everything, to spiritualize science in order to find God in the truth, are the ideal Christianity." Nitsche's Oversoul has been conquered by the self-sacrificing spirit manifested by the peasant of Yasnaya. How much this is due to the teachings of Tolstoy one cannot easily say; and it does not matter, either to him or to any lover of truth. The writer discussed with Tolstoy this subject; this phenomenon of some great truth's or phase of truth's becoming manifest at once in all parts of the civilized world and coming from various sources. The Germans call it "Zeitgeist." The early Christians called it "The Spirit of Truth," which came from their Master.

Looking back over Tolstoy's life, one sees a scion of a wealthy and aristocratic family, questioning the value of the attainments of modern culture while yet reaching out after them, and beginning to try to fathom the great problem of the meaning of life. He leaves the university, quite convinced of the uselessness of what men call science ; and devotes himself to his serfs, who good-naturedly take all that he gives them without showing much appreciation of his efforts, or improvement in their condition. He enters the army, and returns home disgusted by the gore of battle and the curse of war. He writes novels, but turns from the art which was born in him, as useless and immoral. He is repelled by the glitter of society, by its hollowness and its untruthfulness. He looks behind the scenes of the stage on which is played the game which we call civilization ; but sees the mask which the players wear ; and knowing that at heart they are worse than barbarians, that which we call art and culture, he calls stage-trappings. Science he finds to be a lie, religion a superstition, and his own life so empty and meaningless that he is ready to choose death in preference to it. He at last finds the faith that saves him and gives meaning to his life. He finds the Christ and believes in his words; making them the law of his life. He learns to love men and to love them regardless of their class, nationality, or race; and in loving and serving them he is doing the will of God, which is the chief aim of his existence. He gives up his wealth and all those outward signs of refinement by which men of his class surround themselves, and lives that simple, non-resistant life from which has gone out this world-wide influence. A close analysis of his teachings brings one to the following conclusions: He was born with a sensitive conscience. It constantly judged and accused him and none the less his surroundings, making plain to him always the contrast between the ideal and the real; consequently there was a continual struggle going on within him. To quiet his conscience and bring to it that peace which is its true atmosphere have been his

A RECENT PORTRAIT OF TOLSTOY

endeavor " from his youth up," the theme of his writings and the subject of his sermons.

He was accused not only by the wrongs which he committed but by the privileges that he enjoyed and which were withheld from others. The contrast between his comfort, his pleasures, his luxuries, and the poverty of the poor was always a torture to him, and to equalize things was his only desire; to make right the great wrong practiced by his class was his aim in life. It was and is his great regret that he has but partially succeeded in doing so. He saw in the simple life of the peasant a step toward his ideal; in his patience, frugality, industry, and simplicity of mind he found the example he wished to follow; and he began to work with his hands, to mend shoes, fetch the water, and build brick ovens. Little by little he began to discover that the peasant's philosophy of life had in it the germs of the new world order, such as Jesus came to establish; and he condemned all art and culture which did not stand the test of that philosophy. He believed that culture and science served the rich and the strong, that they elevated a few and dragged down the mass of men, which can be elevated only by a return to the simple life as it is in nature, and whose laws of conduct are established in the Gospel of Jesus. In studying his words Tolstoy found that non-resistance toward all evil-doers was the only way of not being dragged to their level and the only way of not increasing violence among men. He believes in his doctrines because they are based upon his own experience and have been drawn from the word of God. They are the laws of his life. This gives him constant courage and a never-wavering faith in the ultimate victory of his teachings. He believes that the Kingdom of God will come, and that it can come immediately into each life as it becomes subject to the law of God. There is in everything he says a note of exaggeration which comes from this sensitive-ness of conscience, and which has often made him unjust to himself and to others. It is as difficult to believe all the things he says about himself, as it is difficult to believe all he says about society as it is, although there is no doubt that he means to see and to tell the truth ; but as it is with men who are careful not to grow stoop-shouldered, that they lean too far back, so he, in his eagerness to tell nothing but the truth, exaggerates and distorts that truth quite unconsciously. There is no doubt that he has tried seriously to live according to his ideal, and there is no doubt in his own mind that he has most miserably failed. " I am no saint," he says, "and have never said that I am. I am only a man who is carried away by his passion, and sometimes and maybe always does not say just what he thinks and feels. Not because I do not wish to, but often because I cannot, and because I either exaggerate or am mistaken. With my doing it is still worse. I am a thoroughly weak man with sinful habits who desires to serve the God of Truth, but who constantly stumbles. If people consider me a man who does not sin or make mistakes, then I must be a terrible hypocrite ; but if they consider me a weak man, then the difference between my words and my deeds is a sign of weakness and not a sign of hypocrisy and lying ; and, above all, then I appear as just what I am, a pitiable but upright man, who has always wished with his whole heart to be a thoroughly good man ; and that means that I wished to be a servant of God." He is as modest as he is honest and his fame has not spoiled him. He does not wave away praise like one who is surfeited by it; he accepts it graciously where it is honestly given, but stifles all attempts at flattery or semi-worship. He never speaks of himself as a prophet or apostle and he has never been known to boast of his achievements; in fact he lacks all those elements which have spoiled many men for leadership. He has neither conceit nor egotism. He does not care to have incense waved before him, and those who come to Yasnaya for that purpose soon find themselves without occupation. And yet one immediately grows conscious of his greatness; there is something defying analysis which marks him. It may be only what the visitor brings with him of anticipation, it may be only the nimbus which fame weaves around his head, and yet it is more than this by far. It may be just that aristocratic breeding which, in spite of himself, surrounds him and makes him different from others of more lowly birth; but if it is that, he has it in a larger degree than any of Russia's nobility, from the members of the czar's household, down. It may be, after all, the exaltedness of the lowly, of which his Master speaks,

which one notices; a strange, spiritual exaltedness which is not akin to the fanaticism of emo-
tional religionists, but which is great and strong
and high because it comes from above and has
its roots deep in the hearts of men. Tolstoy belongs to the few among the great whose glory
does not disappear by contact with them; in fact
he is greatest and noblest at close range. His
speech has none of the hardness which rings
so unpleasantly in his writings, his voice has that
tender tone which woos and wins one; and although it rings out defiantly and definitely it
never grows harsh from anger or his words bitter
from hate. He often hurts one by his scrutiny
because he divines the things one hides from him,
or detects the falsehoods hidden in one's speech.
Perhaps the strangest thing about his personality
is, that one is always under its spell after having
once come in close touch with it. An important
witness to this is Mr. Wolganoff, a wealthy merchant of Moscow, who belongs to the Tolstoy
circle. "Since I have learned to know him he
seems always with me, and in all questions of
life he gives me advice. In moments of spiritual
exaltation it seems to me as if he were with me,

and would tell me just what to do, and I have the satisfaction of always having done the right thing if I follow his advice." Even those who come but to see in him a curiosity go away with the touch of that life clinging to them, and more than one newspaper reporter, after seeing him, has said : "Life seems a different thing now." To explain all this one need not fall into any mystical speculations ; the life of the spirit is the powerful life and the attractive life, and wherever it has genuine expression through a man, there men will say : "It has been good for us to be here." But it is not a life which exhales the perfume of cloistered holiness ; his piety is not musty ; he is too human, too active in earth's affairs ; he is too much of an iconoclast to waste his time in counting beads or mumbling prayers. He does more praying doing God's errands than many men do upon their knees, begging for grace and cake; and he does it at an expense of time and strength which are more and better than fasts and long night vigils. By many hours of conversation with burdened men, and by letters which fill pages, he gives advice to the erring, to the perplexed, and to the weak. It may seem a trivial

example, but to the writer it seems pertinent and
great because it concerned him at a very critical
time in life. He came to Yasnaya Polyana, a boy
with foolish questionings, a stranger without a
line of introduction, troubled by spiritual burdens;
and this man, struggling with great thoughts
and in the depths of a personal grief, gave him
hours in which he taught him, and preached to
him lessons and sermons which lasted through
life. More than once he gave him letters of introduction to friends in Russian cities which opened
doors into other rich lives and made the usually
unpleasant sojourn there a great delight. This
was not done from any selfish motive; this stranger in common with others had nothing to give,
— then, not even a pen which might spread his
praise and increase his fame; and had Tolstoy
known that some day he would attempt to do
this, his treatment might have been less cordial
and his help less freely offered. Yet the writer is
aware that but few can have this personal touch
with him, and that neither this book nor any
other book can bring it; the mass of men must
judge him by his works and his words. His works
— by that is meant his achievements, outside

of the books which he has written — can scarcely
be called great, nor can they be traced very definitely by the historian. Tolstoy has organized
nothing, established nothing, destroyed nothing,
built nothing. He could have done a great deal
even in autocratic Russia ; but he was too much
concerned with his conscience, with gaining his
own peace, to accomplish what the world calls great
things. He had plans for relieving distress among
men, but he saw the causes too keenly and knew
that mere philanthropy was only a palliative and
often did more harm than good. One cannot help
criticising him severely on this point ; it does look
as if he had slipped from underneath the burden
very gracefully ; and it looks like flight, when
a great deal might have been accomplished. He
has not enough sympathy with those who try to
do their little in the world as it is, and who cannot go anywhere into the wilderness and organize a system of their own. Yet he had to see that
even with filthy lucre, something can be done
and that it must and can be used for the saving
of men. His work of keeping from starvation
millions of peasants, and doing it in a systematic
way, ought to have convinced him that there is

some good in money and in organized charity. Yet to the end he regards money as a curse, and is happy when his sons come to him and tell him of the cares and sorrows that it brings ; for then like any ordinary mortal he can say : " I told you so."

Tolstoy's writings are best characterized by saying that there is in them an overwhelming desire for truthfulness. This explains the simple plot of his stories, the naturalness of his characters, the absence of artificial tension ; and it explains also his realism, which to Anglo-Saxon readers is his least desirable quality. He never sacrifices truth to form or to good taste ; his stories are loosely constructed and broken into by his moralizings which are no doubt tedious to readers who are anxious to know whether "they died or were married and lived happily ever after." One cannot persuade him that he might have preached more convincingly by making the sermon less apparent. But as he says : " Sometimes one takes the pen and writes, 'Early in the morning Ivan Nikitsch rose and called his son,' and suddenly one says to himself : 'Old man, why are you lying ? you don't even know such a man as Ivan

Nikitsch.'" He abandoned the story only to return to it; and even now he is writing one in a reminiscent mood, dealing with his life in the Caucasus. When at the completion of his labors his memoirs are written, the critic, whether he prizes them or not, will be able to say of them, in the words of Tolstoy himself: "The hero of his stories, whom he loved with all his heart, whom he tried to represent in all his beauty, and who always was and will remain beautiful, was — Truth."

A word remains to be said about his theology. "God is his father, all men are his brethren." This is the whole of his theological and sociological creed. He tried hard to be an agnostic, and agree with Confucianists, Buddhists, and atheists, and never consider the conception of God. "But suddenly," he says, "I grew to be lonesome and fearful, I did not know why; but I began to realize that I was spiritually degenerating because I was drifting away from God. I began to think how strange it is to say whether there is a God or not; and then it seemed as if I had found him anew. I feared that this assurance might leave me, might grow dull; the main feature of this feeling is that it gives one the consciousness of absolute security, the knowledge that God exists, that he is good, that he knows one, that I am part of him, — one of his children." Tolstoy is an agnostic in regard to the person of Jesus. It does not matter to him who he was, whether God or man; but his word was divine, it was the law of God revealed through Jesus, and in that he has implicit faith; greater faith than most of us who know all about Christ's miraculous conception and who worship him as God. Tolstoy has faith enough to believe that his faith is true, to take upon himself the consequences of it, and to believe in Christ's ultimate triumph. This is what he says: "One more effort and the Galilean will conquer; not in that terrible sense in which the heathen emperor prophesied his conquest; but in the true sense in which he said of himself that he had 'overcome the world.' He will conquer in that simple and reasonable way, that if we have the courage to confess Him, soon all those persecutions which come upon his followers will cease; then there will be neither prison nor gallows, neither war nor burning, neither poverty nor beggary, underneath which the Christian world is now groaning."

Tolstoy has brought that glorious time down to himself; he is not tortured by fear of prison, of sickness, or of death; he is living in the millennium and he says that we also may live so if we let the Kingdom of God come into our hearts. May I in closing repeat what I said four years ago, after a close look into his life? "No; he is not the Christ, but he is a John the Baptist; his gospel is written on the tablets of Moses; his beatitudes have in them the ring of the Ten Commandments. They were graven by the finger of Jehovah, not spoken by the gentle Jesus. But his way of preaching the gospel reaches where our way does not reach; his gospel reaches the lowest, and brings the greatest low. It is a gospel which cannot be misunderstood; it is as clear as noonday. It is a gospel which rouses in man the will, which awakens the soul, and lifts it from its slumber or sloth to a large life and to heroic service. God needs such men in this His day — large men who live above the fog; great men, ready to sacrifice for righteousness' sake. There are too few who do not hedge and halt and temporize, who dare to bear the brunt; too many time-servers, dust-lickers, who grow like mushrooms in the shade, and die like morning-glories in the broad sunlight; too few of us who believe that the gospel is for this time and forever, and who are willing that the Kingdom of God should come within us. This is Tolstoy's great cry: 'The Kingdom of God is within you, and you are to be the pattern after which the kingdom of this world is to fashion itself.' 'Young man,' he said, and they were almost the last words which he spoke to me that evening: 'you sweat too much blood for the world; sweat some for yourself first. You cannot make the world better till you are better.' I have seen many a mountain, — and I love them all, — the Jungfrau in her chastity, Mont Blanc with his icy collar, the Monk, hooded and shrouded, — but there is one rock standing alone above the village of Zermatt, bride of the sky, mother of life-giving waters, now shrouded in mystic clouds, now sharp and clear, standing between earth and heaven. It is the solitary Matterhorn which I love best. The Matterhorn among the great is Tolstoy. I still feel resting upon me those eyes with their life-giving warmth ; I still hear the mellow voice which persistently but lovingly said : 'Young man, you cannot make the world better until you are better ;' and then I said : 'Good-night.' I may never again say to him 'Good-night,' but I trust that I shall say, 'Good-morning.'"